Wisdom and Eloquence

WISDOM *and* ELOQUENCE

A Christian Paradigm for Classical Learning

ROBERT LITTLEJOHN
& CHARLES T. EVANS

CROSSWAY BOOKS

A PUBLISHING MINISTRY OF
GOOD NEWS PUBLISHERS
WHEATON, ILLINOIS

Library of Congress Cataloging-in-Publication Data
Littlejohn, Robert, 1955–
   Wisdom and eloquence : a Christian paradigm for classical learning / Robert Littlejohn and Charles Evans.
     p. cm.
   ISBN 13: 978-1-58134-552-0
   ISBN 10: 1-58134-552-6 (tpb)
   1. Church and education. 2. Religious education—Philosophy.
3. Education, Humanistic. 4. Education—Aims and objectives. I. Evans, Charles, 1967–   . II. Title.
LC368.L58   2006
370.112—dc22   2006001820

CH		16	15	14	13	12	11	10	09	08	07	06
15	14	13	12	11	10	9	8	7	6	5	4	3	2	1

We dedicate this work to

DAVID, KATELYN, KATHERINE, MAURA, PATRICK, ROBERT, AND THOMAS,

all of whom have benefited from a "12-K" liberal arts and sciences education

CONTENTS

ACKNOWLEDGMENTS

THE AUTHORS HAVE many people to thank for their contributions to the extended learning process that has resulted in our writing *Wisdom and Eloquence*. We deeply appreciate the daily "iron sharpening iron" provided us by the faculty, staff, board, students, and parents of New Covenant Schools of Lynchburg, Virginia, Faith Christian School of Roanoke, Virginia, Covenant College of Lookout Mountain, Georgia, St. Timothy's-Hale School of Raleigh, North Carolina, Regents School of Austin, Texas, The Arrowhead University Consortium of Minnesota, and Trinity Academy of Raleigh, North Carolina. We are indebted to the many participants in "forming conversations" at the annual Society for Classical Learning conferences and other similar venues where late-night dialogue has crafted clearer understandings of the daunting prospect of providing young people an education we hadn't the privilege of gaining at their age. Finally, we appreciate the assistance of Steve Britt, Robin Davis, Bryce Carlisle, Melinda Delahoyde, Rod Gilbert, E. Christian Kopff, Renee Skinner, and Paul Ziegler in offering their critical review of the manuscript.

Apart from the generosity of these many colleagues, there could be no *Wisdom and Eloquence*. We offer them our humble gratitude.

introduction

EDUCATIONAL ECONOMICS—
DEMAND AND SUPPLY

WHY ANOTHER BOOK ON education and, in particular, another book on Christian education? Because things keep changing, and we believe that, of all people, Christian educators must be responsive to society's changing needs so that our graduates are prepared to make a difference in the world in which they live. We need to be habitual about improving the quality of the education we provide, not only with respect to *how* we teach, but also with respect to *what* we teach. In the pages that follow, we advocate a timeless system of education, the core of which hasn't changed for centuries and does need not to change in order to meet the changing needs of society. But the ways we go about implementing this system and the emphases we place upon the various dimensions of the system must be flexible to achieve the essential ends of the education we provide.

But what has changed? On a practical level, the economic environment in which our graduates must function is vastly different from that encountered just a short generation ago. With 75 percent of today's workforce being characterized by management guru Peter Drucker as "knowledge workers," the value of raw human intellectual capital is at an all-time high. The demand for mere training in a particular trade or craft has faded with the industrial age, rendering the educational paradigms that catered to such demand obsolete. Instead, the need for men and women who can "think outside the box" pervades the American business culture.

Further, between the mass outsourcing of production and services to other countries and the gradual consumption of American companies by foreign private and government investors, there is increasing demand for those who can function and succeed in a global economy. Meanwhile, the majority of new jobs at home are being generated by small start-up businesses, putting the creative entrepreneur in the driver's seat, not only for the creation of wealth, but for local and regional economic development across much of our nation. And with the bulk of these ventures involving technology, biotechnology, or some other form of applied science or engineering, there has never been a greater demand for a deepening understanding of mathematics and science among American adults.

At the same time, big company scandals involving "cooked" books and insider trading have punctuated the desperate need for a generation of business and political leaders who consider ethics to be as important to the corporate and political landscape as the related economic and political agendas. In short, our nation is crying for leaders who possess the knowledge, skills, and virtues necessary to function, communicate, and succeed in the face of never more rapidly expanding information and communication technologies and never more rapidly changing circumstances.

On a deeper level, truth has changed. That is to say, the way most people in our contemporary culture perceive and process truth is profoundly different from how it was before. Until the dawn of the Enlightenment, faith constituted the major means of knowing truth, but with that dawning, *modernism* reigned supreme as the primary epistemology in American and European culture for two centuries. Perceived truth was apprehended on the basis of rational, empirical, scientific authority. What could be supported rationally must be truth. However, over the last several decades modernism has been supplanted in our global culture by its "nameless" successor, *postmodernism.* For the postmodernist, rational arguments no longer convince, and authority is essentially located in oneself. If I can be persuaded that something is true, then it is truth. The truth I embrace may be different from (even contradictory to) someone else's truth, and that is okay. So believe the postmodernists. As Christians, we may bristle at such thinking, but the sad reality is that our children are terribly vulnerable to the pervasive influences of postmodernism in their world.

So, this significant cultural change poses the deeper educational demand, since education is more about cultural relevance than about attaining economic advantage. We want to prepare our graduates not only to make a living, but also to make a profound difference in the world into which they emerge and in the world that emerges over the course of their lives. We must guide them through the often difficult process of acquiring the skills, knowledge, and virtues necessary for the task.

So what are the essential qualities that our graduates must possess to make the kinds of culturally relevant contributions that we describe? We propose that these essential qualities are the very same as those indicated by St. Augustine of Hippo nearly 1,600 years ago—namely *wisdom* and *eloquence*. Our graduates need wisdom to navigate the murky waters of the current cultural, political, and economic milieu as well as those of an uncertain future. They require more than training for the here and now. They require an education that imbues them with the ability to recognize and understand current trends, the creative flexibility to respond effectively to ever-changing circumstances, and the sound judgment to perceive and champion the highest good for society.

But an education for wisdom is only half the formula. Without the ability to communicate effectively and persuasively, wisdom's benefit is singular to its possessor. Our graduates also require eloquence, especially in a post-Christian, postmodern age when, for many, authority comes not from the Scriptures or from reason but from within. Our wise servant must also be imbued with understanding of and compassion for his fellow humans and must be ready to put his wisdom into action by helping "the many" to embrace the greater good that wisdom offers.

Augustine expressed this most eloquently when he spoke of two cities or kingdoms—the earthly and the heavenly. We must be about the work of both cities at once, looking forward to the heavenly while living in the earthly and bringing to it as many of the characteristics of the heavenly as we possibly can. Such work requires both wisdom and eloquence.

But how will we accomplish such noble educational goals in our students? In his letter to the Romans, Paul urged that his readers not be conformed to this world (the earthly), but that they should be transformed by the renewing of their minds. We allege that from the whole of Paul's writing it is clear that he was not advocating abandonment of the earthly city, but a reversal of roles as to who influences whom. Through renewing their minds, Paul's readers could be transformed and simultaneously become transforming influencers in their world . . . very effective education indeed. Augustine suggested that this is best accomplished through a serious study of the Scriptures and the study of essentially "everything else"—that is through study of God's special revelation of himself to his creatures (i.e., the Scriptures) and through study of his general revelation of himself in creation and providence as well.

What we propose is precisely this: a syllabus that prepares our students for the lifelong journey of independent learning in the Holy Scriptures and *everything* else. We believe that this is best accomplished by beginning with the end of our educational endeavor in view and planning a top-down scope and sequence for the thorough mastery of the classical liberal arts and sciences in Christian context. We must acknowledge that there are other effective ways to educate, but we believe this to be the best of a handful of ways to accomplish our educational objectives. We draw our confidence from the centuries-old tradition itself. We maintain that the classical liberal arts and sciences do not work because they represent a long-standing tradition. Rather, the tradition is long-standing because, as a system of education, it works.

It is worth mentioning that while the tradition upon which we are drawing has its roots in Western civilization, it has its counterparts in Eastern cultures also. Further, this form of education has spread, with Christianity itself, to many nations and cultures throughout the world and has found success in educating peoples of all languages and ethnic backgrounds. The paradigm that we espouse is neither intellectually elitist nor culturally exclusive. We maintain that it is an education for every person and that those schools who extend its promise to a racially, ethnically, and socioeconomically diverse student body will see the greatest benefits of its power.

This book has been subtitled *A Christian Paradigm for Classical Learning*. In our understanding, the expression "classical learning" owes its derivation to the development of the "liberal arts and sciences," beginning with classical antiquity and culminating with modern applications. Those already familiar with the history and application of the liberal arts will detect in this a certain "spin" that calls for an explanation. The liberal arts, as we interpret them for the modern school, include a thorough treatment of the natural sciences; so to say "arts and sciences" is in fact redundant. However, there is such wide misapprehension these days that the liberal arts sufficiently emphasize the natural sciences that we cannot apologize for the double meaning in our nomenclature. Too many have dismissed the liberal arts as an inappropriate paradigm for a technological age, believing it to be a humanities-only approach. So whether our readers understand us to mean the liberal arts (including math and science) plus the "true sciences" of theology and philosophy or whether they understand us to mean the humanities plus the natural sciences is of little consequence. Our message is the same. We will ask, however, the reader's indulgence in our alternate use of "liberal arts" and "liberal arts and sciences" as we address the salient issues related to educating in this rich tradition.

We believe that much in the ensuing chapters will be of great interest and help to parents of school-aged children. But we have written this book primarily with professional educators in mind, not so much as a scholarly work, but as a sometimes apologetic for the tradition, a sometimes historical overview, and a sometimes how-to manual. We have endeavored to address the place of Christian worldview formation, character development, academic rigor, and cultural relevance—together with the concept of "schoolness" and the historical development, explication, and implementation of the liberal arts and sciences for the modern student. Should parents wish, they may be best advised to begin the book by reading "A Message to Parents" in Appendix A. Professional educators will do best to jump right in with chapter 1.

one

THE PURPOSE OF EDUCATION: WISDOM AND ELOQUENCE

IT SEEMS ASTONISHING—archaic, anachronistic—any more to combine one's religious convictions with one's vocational ambitions. But in the history of the human race it has been much more common to do this than not. Modern Western society, the so-called liberal, secular West, is really a historical aberration, not the norm. There are definite benefits to be derived from our current way of life, but they are largely temporal, and they can tend to undermine transcendent commitments. Just because we are the envy of the modern world does not mean we deserve the compliment.

But this book is not a polemic against a decadent West. Rather, it is the expression of a hope-filled goal: that the result of all of the effort we pour into teaching and learning would not only benefit the individuals we educate, but would help our society toward more grace and civility, and toward a universally high quality of life. While acknowledging the truth in the adage that fanaticism can lead one to be "so heavenly minded that he is of no earthly good," we more readily embrace the sentiment expressed by C. S. Lewis that the more heavenly minded we are, the greater earthly good we might do. Though we are not Platonists, we agree with Plato's assertion (which we also believe to be biblical) that the pursuit of transcendent ideals is a sure path toward a satisfying life,[1] and we hope our convictions on both why and how we educate our children will reflect this.

THE WHY

The purpose of all education can be summarized in terms of both meta-physical and practical benefits. The Christian educational life, characterized as "discipleship," is a life of faith-filled learning to be Christlike. The Christian's lifelong spiritual task is to increasingly express one's God-given personality according to biblical norms of truth, goodness, and beauty. The individual metaphysical benefit of this is eternal. The practical benefit of learning to think and live "Christianly" is that every person, regardless of theological conviction, profits by living in a society characterized by these same biblical norms—i.e., a truly civilized society. Though believer and nonbeliever may bicker over definitions, both possess an instinctive judicial sense that signals when they have been treated justly or mercifully.

So, the purpose of Christian education is always twofold. We want our students to grow spiritually, intellectually, and socially, and we want them to foster similar growth in society. Or as St. Augustine of Hippo would have put it, we seek to lead the citizens of earth toward citizenship in heaven, while instilling in them the desire to introduce the values of the heavenly kingdom into the kingdom they presently inhabit. In short, we aim to shape individuals who are both heavenly minded and capable of doing great earthly good.

To be of any earthly good, a person must understand the world around him and recognize what it needs. He must be capable of discerning between what is true and good and beautiful in society and what is not, and he must be empowered to make a difference through perpetuating the former. In short, he requires wisdom and eloquence and not just a façade of wisdom or eloquence. Our activist must understand himself to be the inheritor of a dependable tradition of wisdom (rooted in a transcendent, authoritative source) that he has the responsibility to steward and to articulate to his contemporary world.

We live in a time in which there is no lack of energy for cultural improvement. Despite the broad insurgency of complacency and consumerism, there is a vibrant strain of activism still at work in Western society. From the environment to the sanctity of life, the motivation for reform is alive and well. Such optimistic inclinations are inherited from our cultural ancestors and have been fed by both Christian and non-Christian sources. But the problem facing those who would shape culture today is that the source of true wisdom is constantly in question, even among professing Christians. The education we received ill-equipped us to discern truth, goodness, and beauty because uncertainty and skepticism have become the more common results of education, replacing the optimism and confidence of earlier generations. Yet, the drive to reform and to be open to reform, together with the inner honing device that should guide such reform, is most easily acquired when we are children.

So, the goals of wisdom and eloquence must be clarified and set before each student, parent, and teacher if we hope to succeed in crafting an education that will benefit our society. Augustine noted that true wisdom comprises at least two significant components. First, he said, a thorough reading of the Scriptures and a general knowledge of its contents form the necessary base from which to gain wisdom with any practical value to society. To a Christian, this might seem obvious, but how many churches and schools ignore or seem to have forgotten this basic discipline? How many curriculum guides can verify that when a student graduates he has read the entire Bible or has had its most important stories and theological truths taught to him?

① Study Bible

Augustine's second wisdom component was, essentially, to learn everything else—not entirely or comprehensively, but in a thorough yet moderate manner. He especially recommended broad study of the areas of knowledge that he considered to be "true and unchangeable"[2] like logic and mathematics. These things he ascertained to be "investigated and discovered" rather than invented. The transcendent aim of such pursuits is to discover and to acknowledge the glory of God's creative genius, while the practical, immediate benefits of these studies include an increasing ability to understand, function in, and positively affect the world around us.

② Study everything else

After wisdom, eloquence was the second of Augustine's indicators of a properly educated Christian. Before Homer first composed the lyrical speeches of *The Iliad* in the eighth century B.C., Westerners valued oratorical skill as a sign of great leadership. Augustine had been a renowned professor of rhetoric at the time of his conversion. Though he was raised by a Christian mother in a rural part of North Africa, his recognition of the superior eloquence of the great Roman orator Cicero (106-43 B.C.) had actually prevented him from being able to appreciate the comparatively rustic, Hebraic style of the Scriptures. Augustine's first personal encounter with a highly trained Christian orator, therefore, had profound effect. He found himself compelled to listen to and, finally, to believe the gospel as articulated by Ambrose, the towering bishop of Milan.

We will consider the concept of eloquence as a comprehensive academic objective in greater detail later, but because some might consider it too limited a theme to characterize a school's entire program, it is worth addressing briefly at this point. Ordinarily, eloquence has been taught through the discipline of rhetoric. In the conversation contained in this book, we will limit our definition of rhetoric to its classical articulation—persuasive public discourse. Though we live in an age of fragmented communication, characterized by media-focused sound bites, the necessity of genuine eloquence for cultural influence has not diminished. Even the most unsophisticated audience can sense the difference between a rant and a carefully considered opinion. Though the timeframes allotted for public discourse might have shrunk dramatically since the eighteenth century, what Jonathan Swift called "proper words in proper places" still can have the effect of moving audiences from muddle-headed thinking to sound reasoning or from complacency to action.

Christian education, properly considered, always includes the goal that students will use their schooling to impact the world around them. Not only do we expect our graduates to exercise discernment over their own lives and lifestyles, but we also expect them to be able to persuasively articulate a better way of life to those around them.

We have to be careful, as we educate our students to live "Christianly" in this world, to do more than just teach them how to be a good example to others, should anyone care to look over their suburban privacy fences. Teaching them to think, to discern, and to behave wisely should be coupled with instilling in them a sense of obligation to contend for those same values throughout society. If we believe that Christian living is the fulfillment in this life of what God intends for human beings—if being a Christian is, in fact, "good for us"—then we can legitimately conclude that living in a Christ-influenced society can be good for anyone, even those who do not profess the faith personally. A gracious, articulate citizen who has learned to consider and to communicate within the whole range of human concerns will find it much easier to influence those living in the modern world than will those who have missed this set of skills in their education.

In addition to Augustine's intellectual and spiritual power, there is another reason to look to him and his close contemporaries for advice regarding how to educate today. Augustine lived in a time not unlike our own. In the late fourth century A.D., when Augustine did much of his writing on education and culture, the Roman Empire was at the peak of its power and influence in the world, but its foundations were crumbling. Threatened externally by Germanic barbarians and fractured internally by the meandering politics of affluence, Roman society was precariously poised on the verge of collapse.

In the midst of all this, Christianity was gaining political and demographic strength, but all was not well with this four-hundred-year-old faith. Heresies cropped up like weeds. Political power led to syncretism and moral acquiescence. Generations of energetic believers had come and gone, and many sitting in the churches on Sunday were only nominally committed to the faith of their ancestors. The church tended toward the poles of cultural conformity or cultural separation, with little skill at crafting a uniquely Christian vision of society or making that vision a reality.

Augustine stepped into this malaise armed with a comprehensive perspective on what it means to inhabit two worlds simultaneously. He instructed his flocks and the church at large in the skills necessary to understand and accept the limitations of fallen society while simultaneously energizing the here-and-now with heavenly values. His prescription for wisdom and eloquence resonates into the twenty-first century.

THE HOW

We are proposing what is most appropriately and accurately called a Christian liberal arts and sciences approach to education. We must acknowledge that some have labeled elements of this tradition "classical," but we intend to explicate the tradition on the basis of its historical development as well as its practical efficacy and offer a fresh look at what we believe to be the intended outcomes of the tradition. We maintain that the classical liberal arts and sciences have, for centuries, provided and continue to provide the best way to impart genuine wisdom and eloquence to all who are willing to take up the challenge.

Our approach in this book is to focus on the desired ends or outcomes of Christian education, but a book on education is not much help, nor would it be very interesting without suggestions on how to get the job done. Curricular structures, especially those depending on "old-fashioned," even ancient, ideas about teaching and learning, need some context. If we are proposing an unconventional approach to schooling, we must be able to demonstrate that the ideas we have gleaned from our study and experience have both a historical and experiential basis from which to predict success.

If society needs wise and eloquent leaders, Christian schools should be at the forefront of educating people for these roles. The liberal arts tradition has dependably produced creative and active men and women whose impact on Western culture has been felt for millennia. Christian schools that embrace this tradition and its demands and opportunities will equip their students with practical culture-shaping skills for succeeding generations.

Colleges that still embrace the liberal arts and sciences have long understood the broad scope of their curriculum to be the best preparation for life, the true hallmark of the educated person. This is in contrast to education in the professional or industrial arts, which prepares one for a specific vocation and results in a person's being well trained in a single discipline or craft. Liberally educated people, whose intellectual skills are transferable to the learning of any subject or craft, are increasingly important in an economy in which the average adult changes careers multiple times over the course of his life. This reality starkly contrasts with our parents' or grandparents' experience, when serving forty-plus years in one occupation, even in one company, was commonplace.

But the benefits of a liberal arts education were historically not limited to college students. The truest application of the liberal arts and sciences in their historic context must begin with young children. It is this application that we strongly advocate.

Whenever it begins, the heart of the liberal arts tradition is the core curriculum. The cultural impact of the tradition was made possible by philosophical commitments that supported the view of society proposed by Augustine and his intellectual and spiritual descendants. If we are serious about finding a relevant application of this tradition in the twenty-first century, we have to ask ourselves about our own philosophical commitments. Once we accept the responsibility of this tradition, what should our schools look like? What really distinguishes our schools from others? And what convictions must we as Christian educators adopt to fully engage our students with the liberal arts tradition?

WHAT WE ARE NOT

The dominant theories on education these days are the descendants of modernist educators of the late nineteenth and early twentieth centuries. Cultural icons like Columbia's John Dewey, heavily influenced by the philosophical pragmatism of William James and Charles Peirce, constructed a "progressive" educational mentality that is generally characterized by at least three priorities:

1. It places the student at the center of the educational process, displacing or ignoring the cultural tradition in which he or she stands.

2. It educates students according to deterministic assessments of aptitude prescribing college-preparatory tracks for some and vocational education for others.

3. It generally "vocationalizes" the education process, training students primarily to function in the economy.

John Dewey was a brilliant and complex theorist who remained open throughout his life to his ideas being tested and contradicted. We understand that Dewey himself should not be blamed for the full extent of the drift from traditional principles in American education, but his impact on subsequent theories has been profound. So, while current expressions of "progressive" education cannot always be directly attributed to Dewey, we are convinced that Dewey's work created a seismic shift from traditional American educational theory that has resulted in enormous negative consequences for students and our society.

It is important to note that "progressivism" is not limited to the public educational arena. Most private schools have adopted progressive goals and methods in designing curriculum, even as they justify their existence on the basis of social or spiritual benefits, over against their public school counterparts. We would be hard pressed to state unequivocally that children cannot learn in a progressive environment. Yet it is important to be able to discern the differences that ordinarily exist between schools that have embraced the liberal arts educational tradition and those that have accepted progressive and modernistic assumptions about teaching and learning.

Progressivism, because of its close association with modernism, has grown to be identified with secularism in education. The early progressives were strict secularists—modernists convinced that religious devotion, especially among educators, impedes scientific discovery and social progress. The political necessity of secularization in public schools has only enhanced the standing of progressive theories, because they largely relegate religion to the margins of a student's personhood. Private and even Christian educators, often in order to commend their schools to parents who are content with the banality of conventional education, have increasingly adopted progressive curriculum materials and have incorporated progressive teaching methods into their classrooms.

The inevitable effect for Christian schools that adopt progressive ideas uncritically is a *de facto* dualistic compartmentalization in the curriculum, separating the sacred from the secular. Though it would be unfair to characterize progressively oriented Christian schools as "secularized," still it is a characteristic of un-Christian thinking to separate the sacred and the secular. To the extent that the curriculum structures in our schools do not uphold a consistent, pervasive integration of the sacred into the students' academic and social experiences, we have allowed ourselves to become secularized.

Since liberal arts thinking is currently the minority position in our society, it is easy to think of ourselves as cultural insurrectionists. It is important to remember, however, that modernism overthrew a 2,500-year-old tradition. It, and not the culture we are recovering for our classrooms, is the insurgent. So, against what ideas about teaching and learning have progressive theories rebelled?

PRESUPPOSITIONS

The liberal arts tradition positioned faith squarely in the center of human identity. From the Greek pagans to Augustine, to be a person meant that one is inherently religious. Reflecting Solomon's proposition that "the fear of the LORD is the beginning of wisdom" (Proverbs 1:7; 9:10), Augustine understood religious faith to be inextricable from one's understanding of the world. Differences in opinion over the nature of reality were fundamentally understood to be differences in worldview. The purpose of education in such an intellectual economy was to deepen spiritual understanding through belief in an open, divinely ordered universe as a necessary means of understanding oneself and one's place in the world.

Modern education has replaced faith as a foundational element of certainty with skepticism. It seems ironic, but the result of rationalism or anti-supernaturalism in education is a great deal of uncertainty about what is real. Students in most schools these days are taught a confusing epistemology in which certainty, especially regarding anything outside of the sciences, is looked upon as a sign of intellectual arrogance. Knowing and depending upon a cultural tradition equates with intellectual laziness.

The traditional understanding of human nature has also undergone a radical reconstruction. In the liberal arts tradition, human nature is understood to be immutable. To the Greeks, this meant that the tragedy of the human condition was also irremediable. As Christians, we understand the Bible to teach that fallen human nature, though correctable via redemption, is constant. People are who they are, in every time and in every place, from the moment of the fall of man to the present. So, wisdom gained in 2000 B.C. is wholly relevant to those of us living four thousand years later.

Modernistic views of human nature describe human identity as being in a constant state of flux. Evolutionary psychologists posit that improvements in our awareness of ourselves, symbolized in political changes such as women's suffrage or the abolition of slavery, constitute a change in "consciousness"—a synonym for our nature.

The more radical one's view of the mutability of human nature, the less relevant the experiences and traditions that have preceded us become. For instance, in an age in which there is justifiable moral consensus against one person owning another, there is little or nothing to learn from a writer from an age in which slavery was an accepted norm. So the scholarship and thinking of Thomas Jefferson, for example, becomes irrelevant for the current generation. This was clearly behind

John Dewey's thinking when he wrote, "As a society becomes more enlightened, it realizes that it is responsible not to transmit and conserve the whole of its existing achievements, but only such as make for a better future society. The school is its chief agency for the accomplishment of this end."[3] Dewey isn't simply relieving us of the responsibility to conserve our cultural heritage; he holds us responsible not to conserve most of it. This thinking produces the highest forms of cultural arrogance and inoculates students against the most useful kinds of historical understanding. Who will choose which parts of our heritage are and are not to be conserved?

A third presupposition overthrown by modernism and its educational progeny has to do with objective values. In the liberal arts and sciences tradition, truth, goodness, and beauty have each been understood to be objective categories of knowledge that can be both investigated and known. The Greeks and Romans were, by and large, absolutists. Disagreements among pagans over the nature of truth or goodness or beauty had to do with definitions of their absolute values. Rarely does one find a credible liberal arts thinker who does not assume a basic absolutism. Christianity requires an even higher degree of certainty in that truth, goodness, and beauty are characteristics of God himself. Perfection in each of these arenas is genuinely conceivable because we have seen them revealed and modeled in the person of Christ. So the pursuit of truth, goodness, and beauty is a worthwhile and achievable goal, even with the qualification that we cannot know or practice them perfectly in this life.

Both modernism and postmodernism reject all absolutes. Inherent contradictions between competing visions of truth, goodness, and beauty are ultimately irrelevant. In the abstract, we might enjoy haggling over the notion that "beauty is in the eye of the beholder," but as relativism finds its way into our understanding of truth and goodness, the effects can be horrific. Ethical and moral relativism result directly from the skepticism that accompanies the displacement of faith from our cultural epistemology.

Ultimately, relativism permits each person to define his own version of each of these values, resulting in a world in which six billion people are each encouraged to live according to unrelated and even opposing definitions of notions that are fundamentally important to civic harmony. Carrying such thinking to its logical extreme, Hitler can no longer be morally relegated to the category of "evil," because the category no longer exists. Instead, modern teachers must create for their students a gymnasium of ethical exercises to determine whether the Nazi death camps were, on the whole, helpful or harmful, depending on one's point of view. The end of this persuasion is an educational disaster. In stark contrast, a Christian liberal arts and sciences education rejects such relativism while cultivating in its inheritors genuine wisdom and eloquence, preparing them for culturally relevant living in two kingdoms simultaneously.

two

A RICH TRADITION
IN THE MAKING

THE LIBERAL ARTS, as identified for our purposes, were first canonized in medieval times and numbered seven: Grammar, Dialectic, Rhetoric, Arithmetic, Geometry, Astronomy, and Music. However, they had their origin in classical antiquity as a system of educating those who would be political and cultural leaders in society. The expression "liberal" derives from the Latin *liber* meaning "free." The nomenclature applied to men who were neither slaves nor laborers, each of whom benefited from their own unique systems of vocational training. The evolution of the liberal arts and their application in various cultures had very specific ends in mind. They were preparatory to higher learning and were intended to produce individuals who were skilled, lifelong, independent learners having no further need of tutelage and who, through their continued self-directed learning, would become wise and eloquent servants in their societies.

Irrespective of the cultural setting, the crux of the educational paradigm was always the same—i.e., beginning with the end in view and approaching that end incrementally with each art building upon the other and all leading to the apprehension of the "true sciences": philosophy and theology. The medieval scholar's interest was theology, and the classical Greek's was philosophy and what we call mythology, but both were ultimately concerned with cosmic questions of origins and meaning. In today's academic culture, these "sciences" are far less comprehensive and constitute just two of many specialties or "major" areas of study, but in ancient and medieval times they constituted the hall-mark of a thoroughly educated person. Such a person was ready to bring the wisdom and eloquence gained through his regimen of study to the pursuit and practice of any specialty such as medicine, politics, or law and to contribute to his contemporary culture in meaningful ways.

Despite what may seem a peculiar collection of disciplines and per-haps even stranger nomenclature, the seven liberal arts focused on mas-tery of two broadly defined areas of learning: language and mathematics. Grammar, Dialectic, and Rhetoric were the "language arts," which built in the young scholar the skills and understanding of the meaning, structure, and effective use of language. Through instruc-tion in these arts, the student learned the mechanics of reading, writing, and memory and was introduced to the vast wealth of historo-cultural and technical literature that preceded him. The student learned to apprehend meaning and to analyze content, moral implication, and nuance. He learned to recognize the underlying themes in what he read and committed to memory and to organize his thoughts into salient, coherent arguments and reflections for presentation. Most important, he learned to transfer the skills gained from every area of learning to the others.

Of the "mathematical arts" we readily recognize two as belonging to such a group: arithmetic and geometry. However, at first blush the inclusion of astronomy and music seems incongruous to the modern educator. But the ancient and medieval scholar recognized the interre-latedness of the four, understanding the arithmetic order and rhythm not only of spatial arrangement (geometry) with its implications for the visual arts, architecture, and what we would call the science of natural history, but of the heavens (astronomy) and sound (music). They under-stood the interrelation of each of the four and the interrelation of these to the order and rhythm of the "language arts" as well. While modern theorists acknowledge, for example, the "mysterious" connection between music and mathematics, observing empirically that students of the one often excel in the other, the purposeful interconnection of the liberal arts has been essentially lost as every discipline has emerged in contemporary educational theory into its own silo, having little or no connection with any other.

Not so for the ancients. Writing in the first century B.C., the great Roman architect Marcus Vitruvius Pollio observed:

> The inexperienced may wonder at the fact that so many various things can be retained in the memory; but as soon as they observe that all branches of learning have a real connection with, and a reciprocal action upon, each other, the matter will seem very simple; for universal science [learning] is composed of the special sciences [individual areas of learning] as a body is composed of members, and those who from their earliest youth have been instructed in the different branches of knowledge recognize in all the same fundamental features and the mutual relations of all branches, and therefore grasp everything more easily.[1]

During the Carolingian Renaissance of the ninth century A.D., if not before, the two groups of the liberal arts were identified as "*trivium*" (the three-way crossroad, comprising the three "language arts") and "*quadrivium*" (the four-way crossroad, comprising the four "mathematical arts"). Together the two crossroads of learning were understood to have long been considered prerequisite to the undertaking of all further learning. In the early twelfth century Hugo of St. Victor, ecclesiastical scholar and head of the famous school of St. Victor near Paris, wrote:

> Among all departments of knowledge the ancients assigned seven to be studied by beginners, because they found in them a higher value than in the others, so that whoever has thoroughly mastered them can afterwards master the rest rather by research and practice than by the teacher's oral instruction. They are, as it were, the best tools, the fittest entrance through which the way to philosophic truth is opened to our intellect. Hence the names *trivium* and *quadrivium*, because here the robust mind progresses as if upon roads or paths to the secrets of wisdom. It is for this reason that there were among the ancients, who followed this path, so many wise men.[2]

But of what ancients is Hugo speaking? There were, of course, many, but the evolutionary development of the liberal arts with their component *trivium* and *quadrivium* readily unfolds through a look at the educational practices of a choice few.[3]

In the late sixth century B.C., the Greek philosopher and theologian

31

Pythagoras, best known to us as a mathematician, prepared his students for the "sacred teachings" by means of three progressive levels of learning. These began with oral instruction, followed by "musical education" comprising reading, writing, and memory exercises, and finally the "science of learning" or *mathemata*. For political reasons, which we explain in Appendix B, rhetoric (the art of persuasive speaking) and dialectic (the art of logical argumentation) were soon added to the fledgling canon.

Plato formalized the Pythagorean approach in his "Republic,"[4] identifying an ideal progression in experiencing "the true, the good, and the beautiful" from sensory perception to intellectual perception to intuitive perception. Plato recognized the need to guide young scholars through these stages incrementally beginning, interestingly enough, with music and *gymnasia* (i.e., sport) and elementary linguistic instruction (reading, writing, memorizing, and speaking). These were followed in sequence by the *mathemata*, comprising arithmetic, geometry, and astronomy and culminating in philosophy, which for Plato was inextricably linked to dialectic.

Perfecting the methods of his own master, Plato, Aristotle instructed his young scholars in technical and exegetical grammar using the classic works of literature as fodder for the development of their elementary language skills. Equally emphasized were the twin disciplines of rhetoric (taking the form of the elements of speaking and writing) and dialectic (the elements of logical thought and dialogue).

Among the first-century A.D. Romans, for whom eloquence was the epitome of cultural prowess, rhetoric marked the pinnacle of the preparatory education. The Roman orator Quintilian's instructional regimen began with Latin and Greek grammar, followed by instruction in mathematics and music, and culminated in rhetoric, which included both elocution and dialectic. The Romans, as evidenced by the writings of Cicero, regarded the Platonic notion of ethics and moral integrity as essential characteristics of the rhetorician's art.

By now, our readers can perhaps begin to see that for the ancients, dialectic and rhetoric alternated position as capstone for the *trivium* depending upon the cultural and political demands of the time. In this way, we begin to understand the adaptability of the *trivium* as sufficient for the needs of any age—whether the need is to convince (dialectically) or persuade (rhetorically) one's peers in serving the common good of the culture. Through the mastery of each of the *trivium*'s component parts, the developing scholar gains the necessary tools as Paul (a scholar in his own right) did to "become all things to all people, that by all means I might save some" (1 Corinthians 9:22).

For the apostle Paul and later Christian scholars such as Augustine, the appropriation of the seven liberal arts took the centrality of ethics and moral integrity to an altogether higher level. The arts were considered preparatory, not only for further learning and for service to God and man, but as preparation for eternity. The *trivium* provided the emerging scholar with the tools for apprehending God's special and general revelations of himself through the study of the Holy Scriptures and through observation of nature and history.

Augustine explained in his landmark work *On Christian Doctrine* that the linguistic arts unlocked the treasures of truth contained in the Scriptures. He saw grammar as being the key to understanding the language of the texts, dialectic the means to their hermeneutical interpretation, and rhetoric the guide for dialogue, leading to the cyclical deepening of understanding of the wisdom and beauty of the Creator's self-revelation. The mathematical arts, likewise, drew the human soul heavenward and attuned the mind to fathoming the deep things of God, including order and immutability.

The inheritance from the ancients of the arts, along with philosophical truths, were understood to be the result of God's common grace by which he allowed the discovery (not the invention) of truth by the regenerate and nonregenerate image-bearer alike. The Platonic notion of incremental learning would also be retained as indicated by Richard of St. Victor, one of Hugo's protégés, in the middle twelfth century A.D.: "All arts serve the Divine Wisdom, and each lower art, if rightly ordered, leads to a higher one. Thus the relation existing between the word and the thing requires that grammar, dialectic, and rhetoric should minister to history."[5]

THE SAYERS MODEL

During the liberal arts' recent resurgence as an educational curiosity, many modern evangelicals have gained their understanding of the liberal arts, and especially the *trivium*, by and large from a speech entitled "The

Lost Tools of Learning" delivered by Dorothy L. Sayers to a "vacation class in education" at Oxford University, England in 1947.[6] Sayers was a classics scholar in her own right, an exemplary amateur theologian, a very fine popular author, and one of the early female graduates of Oxford University. Could we but ask her, she would doubtless agree that her rehearsal of the *trivium* and its application was cursory at best, relying heavily on a far better understanding among her contemporary hearers than is typically held by her readers nearly six decades later. In fact, she calls her comments "very sketchy suggestions."

We should make it clear that we have great admiration for Ms. Sayers and would recommend her writings and translations most enthusiastically to our readers. We must also acknowledge that we have, to varying degrees, labored to implement her ideas on education into the curriculum and pedagogy of the schools we have served. However, the experience we have gained through these efforts, combined with our own research into the historical development of the classical liberal arts and sciences and our close reexamination of her own assertions, have led us to disagree with portions of Ms. Sayers's proposal and with the way her recommendations have been attempted at some schools.

Let us first summarize the principles and the paradigm that Sayers proposed. It is important to point out to our readers that this summary is not intended for imitation, but as a starting point for an analytical assessment of the efficacy of the paradigm. In her speech, Sayers acknowledges from the outset that her "experience in teaching is extremely limited" and that her views about child psychology are "neither orthodox nor enlightened," but that the ideas she shares come from "looking back upon [her]self" as a child and upon her own experience as one who has been taught.

Sayers states that the end of education is "to teach men how to learn for themselves." She offers a fairly forceful polemic against the system of educating pre-university students in her day and suggests that the educators of her time had (perhaps borrowing language from Hugo of St. Victor) "lost the tools of learning." She suggests that school buildings and staff should be sufficiently large in order for classes to be sufficiently small for teaching to be effective and that learning outcomes should be verified extramurally by means of standardized testing.

She laments that her ideas are unlikely to take hold since they involve adopting methods that differ strongly from the mainstream of education. In her estimation, the neglected tools of learning are essential "to produce a society of educated people, fitted to preserve their intellectual freedom amid the complex pressures of our modern society."

She declares that the means to these ends is the medieval scheme of education whose syllabus was divided into two parts: the *trivium* and the *quadrivium*. She draws a clear distinction between "modern" and "medieval" education as emphasizing "subjects" and "forging and learning to handle the tools of learning" respectively. Perhaps her most oft-quoted expression is, "although we often succeed in teaching our pupils 'subjects,' we fail lamentably on the whole in teaching them how to think; they learn everything, except the art of learning." Her charge is that when skills are taught, they are "pigeonholed" into instruction in certain subjects, giving examples of grammar belonging to Latin and essay writing belonging to English.

Her view was that the *quadrivium* consisted of "subjects" and that the *trivium* preceded the *quadrivium* and was the preliminary discipline for it. She indicated that the *trivium* alone should be the focus of teaching and learning for the pre-university student. She maintained that the *trivium* consisted of three parts in immutable order: grammar, dialectic, and rhetoric. She further suggested that, of the three, only grammar is actually a "subject" and that the other two are "only methods of dealing with subjects." She also believed that grammar plays a dual role of subject and method, and she coined the expression *grammar* to indicate the rudimentary aspects of the subjects as in "the grammar of history."

Perhaps the most distinctive feature of Sayers's paradigm is her association of the three disciplines of the *trivium* with three stages of cognitive development, which she identifies as the Poll-Parrot, the Pert, and the Poetic. "Now it seems to me that the layout for the *trivium* adapts itself with a singular appropriateness to those three ages: Grammar to the Poll-Parrot, Dialectic to the Pert, and Rhetoric to the Poetic age." While recognizing the difficulty in determining when transitions between one and the next occur, she does offer that the first roughly coincides with ages nine to eleven, the second with ages twelve to fourteen, and the third concludes at age sixteen, when the student will have reached "the school-leaving age," having been equipped with the tools necessary even to be effective leaders in government and society.

Sayers emphasized the need to always use age-appropriate means of instruction and maintained that it is counterproductive, for example, to force rational explanations on a child's mind at too early an age. She acknowledged that questions that indicate a progressing cognitive development should receive a rational answer, but that it is a mistake to assume that a child cannot enjoy remembering things that are beyond his power to analyze.

Sayers's syllabus for which she identifies Grammar, Dialectic, and Rhetoric, not as subjects but as progressive pedagogical phases, is as follows:

GRAMMAR

Primary Faculties (Skills): Observation and memory.

Key Exercise: Latin grammar

Pedagogy: Reciting, chanting, learning by heart: "Anything and everything which can be usefully committed to memory should be memorized at this period, whether it is immediately intelligible or not."

• The grammar of an inflected language, in particular post-classical Latin

• Grammar of a contemporary foreign language

• Reading—narrative and lyric

• English—verse and prose

• Recitation in preparation for disputation and rhetoric

• "Grammar of history" including dates, events, anecdotes, and personalities (e.g., kings of England with pictures of costumes, architecture, and other cultural indicators of the time)

• Geography including factual aspects, maps, natural features, customs, costumes, flora, fauna, capitals, rivers, stamp collecting.

• Science—"natural philosophy" [natural history] including collections, identification and nomenclature.

• "Grammar of mathematics" including multiplication tables, geometrical shapes, and grouping of numbers.

• "Grammar of theology" including Old and New Testaments presented as a single narrative of creation, rebellion and redemption, the creeds, Lord's Prayer, Ten Commandments.

DIALECTIC

Primary Faculty: Discursive Reason

Key Exercise: Logic

Pedagogy: Focused upon the beauty and economy of fine demonstrations of dialectic as well as analytical criticism of less exemplary forms. Use of "subjects" as "grist for the mental mill" to work upon.

- Language including syntax, analysis, and history of language
- Reading essays, arguments, and criticism
- Writing essays, arguments, criticism, and other forms of "precise writing"
- Mathematics including algebra, geometry, and advanced mathematics
- History via analysis and judgment of arguments, enacted laws, and constitutions
- Theology via conduct and morals along with dogmatic theology.
- Geography and sciences as material for Dialectic exercise.
- Examples from daily life, sports, contemporary law, current events, newspaper editorials.
- Research in the form of library and reference research, distinguishing authoritative sources from opinion, etc.

RHETORIC

Primary faculty: Synthesis

Key Exercise: Expression

Pedagogy: Freedom to pursue own interests

- Literature—appreciation more than criticism
- Writing—self-expression
- Specializing in one or two subjects
- Some lessons in subsidiary subjects to keep the mind open to the interrelation of the disciplines (e.g., if specializing in math and science, take some Humanities and *vice versa*)
- Language—discontinue Latin, focus upon modern foreign language
- Mathematics—those with less aptitude may "rest"
- Theology—Included or not, depending upon student interests
- Thesis—culminating written and orally defended work

Sayers, embracing the British concept of education common in her day, advocated two tracks for the rhetoric phase. These depended on whether students intended to attend university (in which case their rhetorical studies would be preparatory for the *quadrivium*, to be tackled at the postsecondary level) or to enter the work force (in which case their rhetorical studies would be more specialized and vocationally focused). In either case, her concern was with the "proper training of the mind to encounter and deal with the formidable mass of undigested problems presented to it by the modern world. For the tools of learning are the same, in any and every subject; and the person who knows how to use them will, at any age, get the mastery of a new subject in half the time and with a quarter of the effort."

Let us first confirm our agreement with much of what Dorothy Sayers asserts and proposes. We agree that one goal of education is for our students to become independent learners and that facilities, staffing, and class sizes should work together to foster effective learning. We agree that using external norms such as standardized tests and other forms of benchmarking are helpful in assuring that our educational goals are being accomplished. We further applaud Ms. Sayers for her call for students to be taught how to think and how to know rather than to be taught subject content only. We also enthusiastically support the notion that ways of teaching should be appropriate to the age and cognitive development of the student. To this end, we see much value in Sayers's "syllabus" for its examples of kinds of things that are appropriately learned at different ages.

However, we take rather strong exception to Sayers's characterization of the *trivium* as a systematic pedagogy and especially to her attachment of the *trivium*'s component parts to her three stages of cognitive development. We disagree with the notion that dialectic and rhetoric are not subjects but are merely methods of dealing with subjects. From ancient times these, together with grammar, have formed the curriculum—not the pedagogy—of the language arts.

In providing us such associations of epistemology and cognition, she at once does us both a great favor and a disservice. Her observation provides us insight into ordering our pedagogy according to our students' learning needs. But she also unwittingly cast in stone for many of her twenty-first-century readers the notion that the classical *trivium* is somehow wed in lockstep fashion to distinct and clearly defined phases in the cognitive and social development of the child. Because it is easy and comfortable for us to fit things neatly into predetermined categories, Sayers's notions have had a compelling appeal. Still, the problem we, as professional educators, have had with this paradigm (and what the ancients understood) is that it does not entirely fit our experience of the child.

A better understanding of the liberal arts and sciences as an educational paradigm, which long preceded Ms. Sayers, insists that we separate the arts from the question of cognitive development altogether. We must adopt the liberal arts and sciences as the curriculum of choice and give careful attention to teaching this curriculum using methods that are sensitive to our students' abilities to apprehend the curriculum's component parts.

We champion, as did Sayers and the ancients, the integration of all the disciplines and the need to purposefully teach our students skills that are readily transferable to other disciplines. We herald, with her, the importance of emphasizing rudimentary knowledge and skills with our youngest students, but we flatly deny that there is any historical precedent or practical necessity for a construct such as "the grammar of history" or "the grammar of mathematics." Because the liberal arts constitute seven foundational disciplines, each with its own rudiments and complexities, we could as readily recommend that students be taught "the astronomy of rhetoric" or "the music of architecture." While it may be clever or whimsical to use such expressions figuratively, the serious use of such constructs undermines the integrity of the liberal arts disciplines. Overall, we believe that the concept has proven far more confusing than useful.

Though she never states it as such, Sayers's readers will likely conclude that the "tools of learning" are the language arts themselves—i.e., grammar, dialectic, and rhetoric. We would instead assert that the tools of learning are the skills that are learned during one's study of all the liberal arts and sciences. Among these skills might be memory, penmanship, phonetic decoding, reading comprehension, computation, critical thinking, analysis, problem solving, research, synthesis, effective writing, public speaking, and sound moral judgment, to name a few. Such skills are not passively acquired but must be purposefully and systematically taught "from end to beginning." This may, in fact, be the most radical notion set forth in this volume. Unlike in the business world, the idea of strategically planning the educational process is foreign to modern educators. But planning the curriculum and pedagogy from the top down is, in our opinion, the only way to ensure the outcomes we intend for our graduates.

The real favor that Sayers has granted the modern Christian educator, and likely the one she intended, is that she got us thinking about how to correct the shortcomings that we all acknowledge exist in modern education. She pointed us to a long-standing tradition that, in her own experience, addressed every one of these shortcomings. Given Sayers's own background and education in the language arts, her heavy emphasis on the *trivium* is not surprising. However, in suggesting that the *trivium* necessarily precedes the *quadrivium* she again confuses the matter. In fact, she contradicts her own assertion by immediately suggesting the study of the mathematical arts and the true sciences for young children. Our assertion is that the ancient and medieval syllabi had students embarking on a lifelong study of all the disciplines from day one.

Consider the experience of learning related by Hugo of St. Victor:

I make bold to say that I never have despised anything belonging to erudition, but have learned much which to others seemed to be trifling and foolish. I remember how, as a schoolboy, I endeavored to ascertain the names of all objects which I saw, or which came under my hands, and how I formulated my own thoughts concerning them, namely: that one cannot know the nature of things before having learned their names. How often have I set myself as a voluntary daily task the study of problems which I had jotted down for the sake of brevity, by means of a catchword or two on the page, in order to commit to memory the solution and the number of nearly all the opinions, questions, and objections which I had learned. I invented legal cases and analyses with pertinent objections, and in doing so carefully distinguished between the methods of the rhetorician, the orator, and the sophist. I represented numbers by pebbles, and covered the floor with black lines, and proved clearly by the diagram before me the differences between acute-angled, right-angled, and obtuse-angled triangles; in like manner I ascertained whether a square has the same area as a rectangle, two of whose sides are multiplied, by stepping off the length in both cases. I have often watched through the winter night, gazing at the stars. Often have I strung the *magada* [a musical instrument], measuring the strings according to numerical values, and stretching them over the wood in order to catch with my ear the difference between tones, and at the same time to gladden my heart with the sweet melody. This was all done in a boyish way, but it was far from useless, for this knowledge was not burdensome to me. I do not recall these things in order to boast of my attainments, which are of little or no value, but to show you that the most orderly worker is the most skillful one, unlike many who, wishing to take a great jump, fall into the abyss; for as with the virtues, so in the sciences there are fixed steps. But you will say, I find the histories much useless and forbidden matter; why should I busy myself therewith? Very true, there are in the Scriptures many things which, considered in themselves, are apparently not worth acquiring, but which, if you compare them with others connected with them, and if you weigh them, bearing in mind this connection, will prove to be necessary and useful. Some things are worth knowing on their own account; but others, although apparently offering no return for our trouble, should not be neglected, because without them the former cannot be thoroughly mastered. Learn everything; you will afterwards discover that nothing is superfluous; limited knowledge affords no enjoyment.[7]

In Hugo's account we recognize the incremental nature of learning while noting the convergence of all the language and mathematical arts, impinging together on the youthful learner. We also detect an appreciation for the interconnectedness of all knowledge and the application of various sensory learning modes, including visual, auditory, tactile, and kinesthetic learning. If we are not careful, we may miss entirely his subtle suggestion that character ("the virtues") is to be learned and, therefore, purposefully taught incrementally, as are "the sciences." Most significant, perhaps, of what we note in Hugo's adult recollections of his youthful experience is the humility characteristic of one who has gained the wisdom and eloquence afforded by a Christian liberal arts education.

A final observation about Sayers will conclude our critique. Because Ms. Sayers challenged the intellectual inconsistencies prevalent in an age of modernism, her emphases were largely upon grammar and dialectic.

Despite her homage to the entire *trivium*, her treatment of rhetoric is minimal. She saw grammar as being developmental to acquiring dialectic prowess—the ability to think critically and posit a salient argument. Our readers will find in this volume a stronger emphasis on rhetoric because, among the language arts, we believe rhetoric to be the culminating discipline for the well-educated student in a postmodern world.

In the ensuing chapters we intend to demonstrate that each of the liberal arts has a proper place in the educational experience of our students at every level of cognitive and social development. The foundations or rudiments of every discipline must have their place in our curriculum and will doubtless be more heavily emphasized alongside the grammar of languages when children are quite young. So while dialectical and rhetorical acumen will emerge in maturing students, the elements of these disciplines, along with those of the mathematical arts and the "true sciences," must be introduced from the earliest lessons and developed incrementally toward their mastery in later years. The same is true of a purposeful nurturing of Christian character in our students. Similarly, it will be necessary to continue to introduce rudimentary principles to mature students when they take up any new discipline of study.

three

WORLDVIEW AND THE
LIBERAL ARTS

SINCE WE ARE PROPOSING A distinctly Christian appropriation of the liberal arts, it is essential to establish a perspective that must inform both our teaching and our learning. Teaching and learning "Christianly" requires much more than adding Bible and chapel to the daily regimen. It requires a whole different way of thinking about education and about life in general. The successful fulfillment of the mission before us necessitates the pervasive influence of a thoroughly Christian world-and-life view as the foundation for our thinking, our doing, and our being.

WORLDVIEW, ENCULTURATION, AND FORMATION

For many Christian educators, the terms *worldview* and *world-and-life view* are in danger of wearing out. The concepts are more than one hundred years old, having been addressed by Abraham Kuyper[1] before the turn of the nineteenth century and popularized in the 1970s by Francis Schaeffer[2] and others. Since those days, nearly every Christian school and college has embraced the terminology and believes *worldview* to be at the core of what it does and teaches. So why should we continue to beat a dead horse? More fundamentally, why does the worldview horse seem dead?

World-and-life view issues may seem "dead," or at least put to rest, not because we have thoroughly mastered the term, but because we have thoroughly misunderstood it and have drastically undervalued it. Adapting Mark Twain's quip about the weather ("Everyone talks about worldview, but no one does anything about it"), for most evangelicals, having a Christian world-and-life view means embracing the "right" positions on important social issues such as abortion or homosexuality. For some it means supporting the "right" political candidate or, in education circles, holding "biblical" positions on such issues as postmodernism or deconstructionism. Such are examples not of worldview, but merely of *positions*.

In reality, even the *values* that lead us to hold such positions emerge from something deeper within us, something visceral, something far more central but far less tangible than positions or values alone. This *weltanschauung*, as Wilhelm Dilthey[3] called it, informs and is foundational to our values and to our sense of institutions such as marriage, government, and society. More than moral or social guidance, it is that inner honing device that colors everything we think, feel, and do. It is what makes women different from men (not the only thing), and it explains why American Christians, for example, don't understand Iranian Muslims or even the French. Worldview is central to our sense of being and is a function of our culture and upbringing.

Oddly, the likelihood of having a genuinely biblical worldview is less dependent upon our personal knowledge of the Scriptures or our parents' knowledge of the Scriptures than it is upon our parents having consistently lived an integrated, Christ-centered life before us. Our world-and-life view is *caught* much more than taught. It is the result of *enculturation* and not just education (theological or otherwise). Enculturation comprises the influences of parents, teachers, pastors, peers, television, music, and even video games (not necessarily in that order). The enculturation process is often passive and barely discernible. It just happens.

So what can educators do to shape or *overcome* a child's developing worldview? Well, when enculturation is purposeful or *active*, we call it *formation*, and we, as educators, need to be about the work of spiritual, cultural, and intellectual formation. Again, formation goes beyond teaching. It includes both the *paideia* (formal instruction) and the *nouthesia*[4] of Ephesians 6:4. It is through formation that we can help reduce our students' susceptibility to the dualism that plagues so many Christians, causing us to separate our religious life from our everyday life.

Such formation occurs when children learn (every day) how Christianity, the Bible, and God himself are integral to *everything*. As Kuyper[5] said: "God looks out across the whole of creation and says, 'there is not one thumb's breadth of it that is not Mine'"—not the physical world; not the spiritual world; not history, science or spelling; not literature, art, or math; not governments, cultures, or societies. It is all his, and we must help our students internalize this enduring truth.

SHAPING THE IMAGE-BEARERS

If we are to exhibit a Christian worldview before our students, it must include *them*. Our theology needs to extend to our notions of children, and especially of children as students. This mind-set recognizes each student's value as one who is created in the image of God, and it encourages the creative energy that stems from each child's image-bearing quality. This worldview mind-set engages *each* student as a child of God in need of *discipleship*.

Christian teachers occasionally find that the worst hellion in the class turns out to be the next great Christian leader. We don't produce these leaders (that is the work of the Holy Spirit), but we can encourage this potential by reminding ourselves and each other that all of our students, whether they profess faith or not, are fashioned in God's own image. As image-bearers of the Creator, each student is worthy of respect and is deserving of the challenge to manifest his God-given talents to the Creator's glory. Each student is God's gift to his school and to his teachers.

The image-bearers of a creative God are themselves creative by nature; so creative thinking needs to be encouraged, directed, and shaped, not stifled. We are *teachers*, not merely facilitators of indiscriminate discovery as the educational establishment would often have us believe. But we must teach in ways that bring to expression the creativity that God has instilled in each of his children. Artistic, mathematical, scientific, literary, and even theological creativity are signs of a growing disciple and of a healthy learning community. Encouragement of such creativity is indicative of a culture in which the divine, image-bearing gifts of each student are valued.

The Christian school, staffed by Christian teachers who are bound by Jesus' Great Commission, has *discipleship* at the core of its responsibilities. This concept is articulated differently in each tradition, from the Baptist expression of a closer walk with Christ, to the Reformed mandate of covenantal child-rearing, to the Lutheran concept of strengthening faith planted in baptism. If we provide a whole class of students with instruction that is intended to strengthen the believing student, even the nonbelieving student benefits, having the opportunity to be drawn closer to Christ. Every time we invite students to thank God, to recall his mercy, or to use his gifts, we invite them into a relationship with Christ. We have been blessed over the years to have had a number of students first profess faith in Christ when enrolled in classes intended to strengthen faith, not just initiate it.

Contrary perhaps to common perceptions, Christian teachers should treat students *inclusively*, not distinguishing in our treatment between believing and nonbelieving pupils. If we hold students at spiritual arm's length, we predispose them toward remaining "outside the camp." If, however, we embrace them and include them in the fold, they are encouraged to identify themselves with the community of faith and to confess that faith along with the rest of the community.

God, the ultimate timekeeper, knows what providence these children will realize. It would be a tragic mistake to withhold discipleship from one who, years hence, exhibits powerful evidence of God's grace in a life of late-found faith. So, recognizing God's sovereign grace and maintaining a humble dependence on God to know the spiritual condition (present and future) of every child, we welcome the call to be instruments of redemption in each life—the Potter's understudies, shaping each of God's image-bearers for his ultimate glory.

THE IMPORTANCE OF A PARADIGM

In the earliest period of my development as a "thinking Christian" I (Littlejohn) resisted systems. I valued biblical theology (and still do), which ventures to extract theological truth from individual texts of the Old and New Testaments, while dismissing systematic theology, which attempts to order theological truths from the whole of the Scriptures into a coherent system of theological perspective. My own bias in this respect resulted from my suspicion that any system is subject to the worldview bias of the theologian. I still believe this concern to be well substantiated and something to be carefully guarded against. However, in recent years I have had to repent of my earlier partiality and recognize that without a coherent system there is little hope of believing or living *consistently.*

In reality, every human being functions according to some kind of theological system—some more complex or ordered than others. Some have described a person's worldview as a "structural framework or grid" through which each person views every aspect of life. John Calvin[6] urged that we use the Scriptures in this way, as a kind of "spectacles" through which we view the world.

We all have such grids or frameworks. No matter who we are, we all view life through spectacles such as conservatism, liberalism, secularism, or evangelicalism. But teaching that successfully integrates faith with life and learning depends on a coherent basis for and consistent method of thinking. However, for even our more sophisticated students, an abstractly labeled philosophy like Calvinism or Thomism just doesn't suffice as a personally relevant worldview identity.

A more concrete approach, and one that has replaced the other options in my own spiritual formation, is most clearly stated as "Creation-Fall-Redemption-Consummation" thinking. This avenue to ordering one's worldview begins with the understanding that all human beings are created in God's image and for his glory and that "in the beginning" God gave mankind responsibility—to subdue the earth and to exercise dominion over his creation. This is often called the creation mandate, and some, by extension, have called it the cultural mandate. It was man's original charge in a perfect, pre-fallen world to cultivate all that was good in creation, including the natural world and the fledgling socio-cultural institutions of family and community, and to sustain this perfection through purposeful effort. Pre-fallen man had the capacity to do wrong (if he didn't, there would have been no Fall), but his charge was to uphold the right by exercising just dominion over all that was.

Subsequent to Creation, the Fall described in Genesis affected not only the soul of man but also the whole of creation. As a consequence of the Fall, people need redemption, but so does every other aspect of creation, including the physical universe and all social constructs and institutions (such as marriage, churches, governments, and, yes, schools—even Christian schools). Human relationships of all sorts are fallen and need to be redeemed. Such understanding leads to greater humility and acceptance as we acknowledge ourselves and others to be broken vessels ("cracked pots") who don't quite meet God's pre-Fall production standards.

Further, we know that Christ himself accomplished human redemption through his atoning work on the cross. Christ alone has the ability to repair and restore the broken/fallen soul. But how does he accomplish the redemption of the rest of creation? How does he bring restoration to human institutions and to nature itself? He does it through us, his image-bearers, who serve as his agents of redemption, performing redemptive or "redemption-like" acts in our various realms of service. Because of God's *common grace* (that favor through which he allows all persons to live and function and affect the world around them), non-Christians often unknowingly act as Christ's redemptive agents through, for example, political action or medical science. Believers, however, should be his conscious agents of redemptive change in the world.

This Creation-Fall-Redemption perspective has far-reaching consequences. We all make decisions every day, and many of our decisions affect other people and the institutions of which we are a part. More often than not, teachers, administrators, and board members make professional decisions on the basis of intuition or experience alone. If we remember to see ourselves as part of a fallen creation and even our ability to make decisions as being affected by the Fall, we might be more humble and careful to gather opinions, information, or data pertinent to our educational, administrative, or discipline decisions, for example, before making them. In this way we may facilitate redemption in the circumstance at hand rather than perpetuating fallenness. Such redemptive acts, however small, affect individual and institutional success for the better and improve human relationships in the process.

Not only does this worldview structure have the potential to influence our personal interactions and responsibilities, but it affects our understanding of larger societal issues as well. For instance, many

Christians believe that genetic engineering is tantamount to "playing God" and should be avoided. As a scientist, I (Littlejohn) understand my work as that of an agent of redemption, bringing improvement to a biological world corrupted by the Fall. Through the marvelous power of genetic engineering, we are able to improve food production and human health. Of course, we must always weigh such opportunities against biblical and ethical norms, but applying this perspective could radically change our "Christian" view of such topics.

Further, it is easy to see countless ways in which such thinking can bring real insight to the study of all academic disciplines. Such insight comes as God employs our assistance to reveal himself to his image-bearers by his *general revelation* (his revelation of himself in *creation*, through our study of nature by means of the natural and social sciences as well as the arts, and in *providence* through our study of history and anthropology, for example). As we serve as his agents of redemption in the classroom and in daily life, God wipes away bits of the smudging that clouds the view that others have of his image, reflected in the darkened mirrors of our lives and in those of our students.

Finally, while our redemptive acts are useful, they are nevertheless imperfect. No one but Christ can bring perfect redemption to any aspect of a corrupted creation. When he, through his own power, brings about a new heaven and a new earth, then the paradigm is complete. Then we will know the *consummation* of the redemptive work that he has chosen to begin and continue through us. As the apostle Paul says in 1 Corinthians 13:12, "For now we see in a mirror dimly, but then face to face. Now I know in part; then I shall know fully, even as I have been fully known." This is the final and triumphant piece of the paradigm—consummation.

POSSESSING WORLDVIEW THINKING WITH HUMILITY

In this chapter we have examined our responsibility as educators to view each child as God's image-bearer and to be intentional in shaping our students' spiritual, intellectual, and cultural lives. We have suggested that worldview thinking is "caught" more than it is taught, thereby emphasizing the importance of modeling Christlike behavior and the habits of thinking "Christianly" before our students. We have reminded ourselves that worldview is central to our task as teachers, providing the structure for our instruction and the context of everything our students learn from us.

Despite these important and positive aspects of worldview thinking, the possession of worldview "filters" can have its downside. To a man with a hammer, everything can look like a nail. We may be led to wrong conclusions and actions through the stubborn (even unconscious) application of our own world-and-life view to many of life's situations. It is important to realize that our personal world-and-life view (from which issues a constant stream of ideas) needs, with every thought, to be brought into captivity to Christ. Old dogs can learn new tricks, and as thinking Christians and educators (since we teachers shall face the greater judgment) we must be diligent to pursue truth with humility. If we are honest with ourselves, we will recognize that the line between good and evil more often runs through things, ideas, and people (including ourselves) instead of running between them. The close, objective scrutiny of all created things (animate and inanimate) uncovers the telltale evidences of the Fall in the redeemed and—by God's grace and with our concerted efforts, we pray—evidence of progressive redemption in the fallen.

I (Littlejohn) have always loved what a wise pastor said to me more than twenty years ago: "I know my theology is wrong. I just don't know where it is wrong." This typifies the kind of spiritual and intellectual humility that acknowledges the effects of our fallen condition, a condition that limits even our ability to perfectly understand God's special (scriptural) and general revelation of himself to us. We must read, pray, discuss, and examine our ideas and attitudes, and we must remain open to the work of the Holy Spirit. He is incrementally perfecting our worldview by helping us to bring our thoughts captive in obedience to the one who does have his theology entirely right—Christ our Lord. In this way, we not only model Christlikeness to our students, but we genuinely stand ready to be influenced by a more accurate understanding of who God is and how he works, both in us and in those whom our lives touch every day.

four

THE COMMUNITY OF FAITH
AND LEARNING

THE EDUCATION THAT WE propose will of necessity be characterized by high standards of academic achievement. It will require rigor on the part of the curriculum and hard work on the parts of student and faculty alike. But such an education could take place in many settings. While essential, academic success alone falls short of the culturally relevant educational experience we intend for our students. Worldview formation and character development are critical dimensions of such an education, and these, to a large extent, depend upon the cultivation of a learning environment consistent with the kind of education we offer.

Since character development is to be among the goals of the education we provide, our first commitment must be to integrity in the *institutional* character we portray. Integrity of character in the institution and in the people it comprises will naturally lead to integrity in the process of character development. But Christian schools often suffer from a case of identity confusion because they are not as well understood as are other God-ordained human institutions. We each tend to ascribe to schools the characteristics of another, better-understood institution, depending on our own frame of reference. Some tend to see the school as a "family," while others see it as a "business." Both are incorrect. Further, Christian schools, in particular, are often confused with churches, and, depending upon the comparison with which we are most comfortable, we expect the school to behave or perform like a family, a business, or a church, and we suffer some confusion when it does not.

In reality, schools are schools. They hold a unique position in God's order for human institutions and are best served and serve best by exhibiting characteristics and behaviors that are unique to schools. Since schools are not families, they should not perform the functions of the family. This has been especially confused in modern times as schools have taken on the responsibility of training children in the basics of human health or sex "education," or that of providing extended care or before- and after-school meals. Similarly, some Christian schools confuse themselves with church, for example, by evangelizing, serving Communion at chapel, re-creating a youth-group culture, or insisting that teachers meet the biblical qualifications of elders. While denominational schools may legitimately choose to include certain of these, it must be recognized that such practices are the church's domain. Schools must guard against the likely exclusionary effects that "church-like" practices may have on students and families from other branches of Christ's church.

The mission of the school, in short, is not to evangelize, not to parent, not to generate revenue, but to *educate*. As such, every school exists as a community of people who gather to pursue the twin purposes of teaching and learning; so schools are communities of teaching and learning. When this mission is pursued in the context of the Christian life of faith, a higher purpose is achieved—that of *discipleship*. Ideally, when Christians gather in such communities, the teaching and learning is integrated with faith, and the education that occurs leads to transforming young hearts and minds to be more Christlike. Such schools are *communities of faith and learning*. It is within this context of "schoolness" that we are best able to achieve our educational ends of imparting wisdom and eloquence and to keep our focus on our goal of emphasizing worldview formation, character development, academic quality, and cultural relevance.

Unfortunately, the notion of truly integrating faith with any practical enterprise is rare these days. Because of this, constructing a community that inextricably combines faith and learning is at once natural and daunting. It is natural, in that the biblical worldview can be logically established as both an epistemological (how we know) and a relational basis for teaching and learning. The process is daunting because the demands of Christian faith are total, and every aspect of our life together in school reflects our level of commitment to this integration.

ETHOS

If, as we shall suggest shortly, the curriculum is the scholastic organism's "skeleton" that provides form and capacity to bring the school's mission to the classroom, ethos is the "heart" of the school community. This is where the community of faith and learning finds its most thorough expression. By ethos, we mean the essence or the "feel" of the school as a community of faith and learning.

A few years ago I (Evans) read a series of articles on the "best high schools in America," published in *U.S. News and World Report.* One of the schools featured was a Jewish school for girls in New York City. As I read this particular article and looked at the pictures, I was struck with a cataclysmic thought: *Those girls look happy!* Stepping out into the hallway of my own school, I watched my high schoolers make their way from class to class. They looked earnest and hurried and a little anxious, perhaps productive, but not happy. I realized my school had an ethos problem, and something had to change.

In contrast, I (Littlejohn) have perhaps been paid no greater compliment as a head of school than that offered by a visiting delegation to our school from another state over a decade ago. After much reading and from attending national conferences that promoted and explicated the particulars of a "classical" education, this group of parents and professional educators had grown disillusioned at the prospect of founding such a school. They had come to believe that the approach was too rigid and unfriendly to benefit "normal" children. As a last-ditch effort, they scheduled a trip to Virginia, and after a day of observing, they assembled in my office with smiles beaming from their faces. They were thrilled to learn that what they had been convinced was a superior approach to educating could be administered in an atmosphere of acceptance, grace, and inclusion rather than in the manner they had previously observed. Quite simply, they appreciated the ethos of the school.

From the moment a student is enrolled in the school until he departs, the ethos of the community of faith and learning colors the entirety of his experience as a student. From classroom to locker room, from chapel to recess—every circumstance has an enculturating effect on our students. Every personal sensory and relational encounter leaves a lasting impression. Some are major, others minor, but they all define our students' experiences, and each will contribute something to the result that our students will call their education.

Ethos is the inarticulate expression of what the community values. It includes the quality of the relationships within the school, the traditions, the professional comportment, the approach to classroom management, the out-of-class decorum, the aesthetic personality of the school reflected in the student and faculty dress codes, the visual and auditory imagery, and the physical plant itself. And ethos is interfused with the academic culture including curriculum, pedagogy, faculty preparation, and student learning. Ethos is the way in which the school expresses (or doesn't) truth, goodness, and beauty through the experiences of every person who enters our halls.

RELATIONSHIPS

Decades removed from our own primary and secondary school experience, it is interesting to note how little we recall of the day-to-day classroom experience. The dominant academic influences that we can recall have more to do with the teachers and administrators who valued us than with sophisticated pedagogical plans. Even easier to recall are the friends with whom we played and sang and traveled and built homecoming floats—and, oh yes, studied.

The fact is that by the time we finished high school we were fully in the throes of adolescence and, despite brief forays into the future to take an aptitude test or to select a college, our lives were about the here-and-now. Children and teenagers have an amazing ability to remain rooted in the present, even as the present continuously runs out from under their feet. For all of our attempts to form them into men and women for the future, their natural inclinations focus on today. And today—that party, the crazy stunt in chemistry, the breakup note stuck in the locker—is what they most often remember. The challenge for the Christian educator, while shaping the emerging adult in our students, is to simultaneously capitalize on the here-and-now.

Juggling these two realities can be a colossal challenge. But before we despair of ever being able to achieve any kind of focused purpose in our students, let us remember this: while there is much within the environments of our schools that we cannot control, there is an awful lot that we can and should. To the extent that we do, we take students beyond the effects of mere enculturation and grant them the lasting gifts that result, as we have earlier said, from spiritual, intellectual, and cultural formation, all of which contribute in wonderful ways to the emerging character in our fledgling image-bearers.

But, where do we begin? Every relationship—whether between teacher and student, student and student, teacher and teacher, teacher and administrator, or teacher and parent—*every relationship* should be characterized by mutual respect and by recognition on the part of each that the other is an image-bearer of the Creator. Students should, of course, be taught and expected to demonstrate a respectful attitude toward the adults in the community, even as they are encouraged to express opinions that are contrary to those espoused by their seniors. This demonstration of respect will take different forms in different parts of the country and, to some extent, from school to school in the same region (e.g., "yes Sir," "yes, Mr. Smith," or simply "yes"). Nevertheless, the guidelines for respectful response and interaction should be school-wide, should follow the principle of civil discourse, and should be reinforced consistently.

It is equally important for teachers to respond toward their students with genuine respect, not belittling their opinions, their input, or their persons. Students should know, even when being corrected for academic inaccuracies or disciplined for inappropriate behavior, that their teachers are "for" them. That they are respected as fellow image-bearers should never be in question. Faculty who intentionally see themselves as partners with students in learning and growing provide themselves with a tremendous opportunity to form their students. Similarly, we have found over and over that students who are given responsibility to help shape the culture and traditions of their school tend to respect and participate in the community more enthusiastically. Student ownership certainly has its risks, but learning to manage those risks and to recover from mistakes is part of what can make Christian schooling such a dynamic process.

Teachers and administrators need to always display mutual respect as professionals and fellow members in the community of faith and learning. It should go without saying that no member of the school community nor his opinions should be disparaged in even the slightest way in front of students, parents, or colleagues. Differences of opinion may be acknowledged, but only in ways that reinforce the value even of opposing opinions in contributing to "the great conversation." Persistent differences should be boldly addressed, face to face, with grace and with a view toward protecting the best interests of the school community and particularly those of its students. Whether professionals address one another by titles at school is a matter for each school to consider, but any policy must have wide acceptance, and the core relationship among the school staff should be one of warm acceptance of each other as equal members of the community.

Students should be held strictly accountable for treating one another with respect. Few things disrupt the harmony of the school environment more than toleration of mistreatment of students by their peers. Nothing angers parents more than the physical or verbal bullying of their child, and no excuse can justify or pacify. Better a teacher or administrator face a bear robbed of her whelps than to face a mother whose child has been wronged—especially when the school has no clear plan of action to address the problem. Because teachers and administrators cannot hear or see everything on campus, students should be taught and rewarded for valuing the difference between "tattling," a power play that calls attention to another's behavior from a motivation of personal gain or retribution, and "bringing wrongdoing to light," which (ideally) is motivated by a desire to preserve peace and to help others learn to get along. There may be a fine line between the two in the mind of the student, but with consistent reinforcement, the difference can be learned and practiced.

A similar principle applies to matters of honor. America's famous universities all had honor codes at one point or another, and many private schools have imitated the form by adopting codes against lying, cheating, and stealing. Most honor codes contain the condition that if a student knows that another student has behaved dishonorably, in a way that will bring shame to the school or that undermines the integrity of the academic community, he or she is obliged to bring that offense to light. Well-known colleges such as the service academies, the University of Virginia, and Davidson College still have strict honor codes and promote their zero-tolerance policies as positive distinguishing characteristics. Another common component of honor code programs is a student-led honor council, which adjudicates cases in which students are accused of lying, cheating, or stealing. Again, there are risks to student ownership, but the rewards of a well-designed program can have a powerful impact on all involved.

Discipline, like instruction, must often be individualized. What works with one student may not work with another, and every student "deserves" the special attention of disciplinary measures that are effective for her or him. The challenge, of course, is to ensure that disciplinary measures are just. We say "just" and not "fair" since fairness suggests equality and "sameness" for all. Instead, discipline should "fit the crime" for any given student in any given situation.

I (Littlejohn) recall some years ago a teacher who had cautioned a student about a repeated infraction numerous times. Finally, in frustration she warned the student that if he repeated the infraction he would not be allowed to participate in the coming field trip with the rest of the class. The student couldn't resist the challenge, and true to his teacher's word, he was excluded from the field trip. In this case, the mother very cleverly made me aware of the "injustice" by volunteering (in feigned support of the teacher's decision) to keep the child in the classroom reviewing his lessons for the entire day. This "partnership" between parent and teacher was not successful. After hearing more details, I counseled the teacher, who had long since realized the over-severity of her choice of discipline, that an admission of making a wrong decision and remedying it is actually a good lesson in modeling humility and justice to our students. In contrast, a partnership that may prove quite successful is for teachers to ask parents for suggestions on effective disciplinary measures for their child. "What does your child dislike doing?" is a very legitimate means of discovering the one thing that will work with a wayward student.

In general, teachers should not exacerbate a potential difficulty with their students by heaping rule upon rule in the classroom. Some Christian educators have quipped, "when God gave us commandments, he limited it to ten," while others feel that lengthy lists of rules are entirely appropriate. We recommend a short list of schoolwide rules and that teachers identify no more than five classroom rules and teach them to students along with initial consequences during the first week of school. We should be sure when we discipline that it is for a clear infraction of the rules rather than for the forgetfulness that can occur when a list of rules grows too long. However, one of the rules for every classroom might well be, "follow the instructions given for every exercise or activity." This rule tends to cover "a multitude of sins."

Discipline in the Christian liberal arts school should achieve a balance between grace and responsibility. The integrity of relationships is one of our top priorities; so the desired end of all discipline is the reconciliation of strained relationships between students or between students and their teachers. Facilitating a biblical pattern of confession, repentance, forgiveness, restoration (including just reparations), and reconciliation should always be our goal. Faculty members ought to be empowered to help students maintain their relationships with each other and their teachers as they should, with ready support from administrators and parents.

As we teach students God's commands, we are helping them learn obedience by comparing their behavior to biblical requirements, commending them when they are obeying God's commands and correcting them appropriately when they fail to obey. We also teach students to live within conventional social standards. So even though the Bible does not tell us everything students should do, we legitimately ask them to demonstrate their knowledge of ordinary courtesies—courtesies that will commend them to others as they make their way in the world beyond the walls of the school.

Openness should characterize the relationships between teachers and parents. There should be a general transparency between teacher and parent concerning the child, and a spirit of teamwork should be cultivated. We have told many parents, "We won't believe everything your student says about you if you won't believe everything they say about us," but some things said by students should not be ignored. Teachers are well advised to pursue good relationships with parents early, so that ensuing issues may be more readily addressed and more positively disposed. Administrators or faculty supervisors who become aware of conflicts between parents and teachers are wise to meet with both parties together to resolve issues quickly and accountably, before matters have an opportunity to get out of hand. If teacher and parent arrive and depart such meetings together, there is no suggestion to either that collusion exists between the administrator and the other.

A final observation about openness in school-related relationships is that gossip can poison a community and lead to deep and irreparable relational damage. It is hard to get toothpaste back into the tube. In principle, teachers, parents, and staff should be urged to address concerns about anyone with the person in question. This is the biblical principle of Matthew 18 and James 4:11, and every effort to educate the school community in this regard will be time well spent. A wise response for anyone hearing complaints is to ask the bearer of tidings, "What did that person say when you spoke with him (or her) about your concerns?" Without a positive reply to this question, the next appropriate response can be, "Why don't we go and see her together?"

School heads and school board members often hear complaints from teachers and parents about others. Most leaders tend to be problem-solvers who like things to run smoothly, but a basic management principle needs to guide our responses to conflict within our schools: Decisions should be made and problems solved at the lowest possible level within the organization. A commitment to this principle helps to make everyone in the school equally responsible for harmony and basic Christian charity. Leaders who become overly involved in conflict resolution may unintentionally enable others to abdicate their own responsibility to think and act like mature adults committed to the integrity of faith and learning. Leaders must learn the difference between holding others accountable for conflict resolution and becoming overly involved in resolving any little conflict that floats across their desks.

TRADITIONS

Few things in a student's experience better help him or her identify with the community of faith and learning or leave a more lasting impression than traditions. But unless a school has a decades-long set of traditions that have remained in place over the years, it is likely that traditions will change with generations of students and leaders. The easiest place to establish traditions that will last is in ceremonies involving the whole school community. Convocations, baccalaureates, commencements, and chapel services all provide an opportunity to celebrate and promote the essential characteristics of the school's mission.

Social traditions are also crucial to giving students a sense of identity within the school. Whether proms or banquets, pilgrim feasts or carnival days, such events reflect our students' childlike (not childish) or adolescent values. Remember, schools are for kids, and the social activities that our schools provide must seem relevant at any given age to what kids value while also instilling in them the school's values. Traditional events such as these can also provide opportunities for partnerships between older and younger students to form and grow as upper-school students partner with lower-school students for a day of whole-school special activities. Such relationships can themselves form the basis for traditions. Some schools have paired whole classes (tenth with seventh for three years) for mentor-protégé activities and "passing the mantle" as the senior class leaves and the rising tenth grade becomes the mentor class taking on the rising seventh grade as their protégés.

CO-CURRICULAR ACTIVITIES

For many of our schools, traditions will begin to emerge around our athletic programs and other co-curricular activities. These are non-academic areas of student activity that the school sponsors because they are consistent with, if not essential to, its mission and identity. The challenge in developing co-curricular activities is to plan them so that they enhance, rather than detract from, the school's purpose and its larger objectives for each student.

An example from one of our schools might illustrate what we mean here. At Regents School of Austin, one of the five strategic objectives for student experience has to do with developing cultural leadership. Given the state of cultural leadership today and its prerequisites, the school has identified three basic areas of accomplishment that will promote students into culture-shaping roles: poetic, artistic, and athletic. In this rubric, "poetics" has to do with competitive co-curricular activities that employ skills derived especially from the liberal arts, like mock trial, debate, and chess—intellectual or persuasive exercises. Artistic activities have to do with the creation and presentation of artistic works in exhibits, plays, concerts, etc. Athletics has to do with interscholastic athletic competition in the sports the school sponsors.

In each instance, the formal academic curriculum contributes to the co-curricular activities that move students out of the classroom and into contact with the community. In today's world, politicians, artists, and athletes are our cultural icons, and these poetic, artistic, and athletic exercises and contests prepare students to position themselves in these spheres of cultural influence.

STUDENT DEPORTMENT

This old-school term has a lot to say about our goals for our students. How students are expected to behave and present themselves at school is a key reflection of how seriously we take the responsibilities to build and preserve school culture and, in the process, student character development.

Knowledge of the Scriptures (when catalyzed by the Holy Spirit) leads logically to faith in Christ, which in turn requires a lifetime of learning to love and obey God's commands. Obedience produces what we call these days *character*—what the apostles often called *godliness*. When I can confidently predict that my student, having developed an intentional habit of obedience over disobedience, will obey in this or that circumstance, I can credit him with character. Every moral choice has a rationale behind it, and one indispensable task of a Christian education is to constantly expose that rationale, whether for good or ill. Our schools should be laboratories dedicated to the constant analysis of choices that either demonstrate godliness or expose the hypocrisy of our convictions.

Character, as it becomes evident in students' habits, provides for opportunities to enjoy the Holy Spirit's work in those students who are being genuinely converted. There is a difference between the character a student exhibits as he merely learns not to complain about the rigors of becoming educated and the genuine fruit of the Spirit that provides him with joy in the midst of his academic trial. The mark of a truly Christian school is not necessarily to have classrooms and hallways crowded with students who consistently and predictably embody the fruit of the Spirit. Rather, it should be a place in which those spiritual indicators are celebrated and modeled by the teachers, administrators, and coaches whom the students will emulate.

Dress is one of the more visible elements of deportment. Both authors are enthusiastic proponents of uniforms in school, but any student dress code must meet the criteria required for any other cultural component and not constitute a contrivance. Too many private school administrators have tried to impose an artificial culture on their schools through the superficial method of clothing. In laid-back Austin, Texas, a school uniform that keeps kids buttoned up and starched would be an unnatural attempt to force another region's values on kids whose professional parents wear jeans and sandals to work. In contrast, allowing kids to wear denim every day in Atlanta or New England might seem equally out of place. The great thing about uniforms is that they don't have to be formal, just uniform. There may be merit in distinguishing certain days (e.g., chapel days) as dress uniform days and others as casual uniform days, while treating the students to the occasional "free dress" day on special occasions. Still, schools should consider the broader culture of which they are part in determining student dress.

Another thing to keep in mind is that times do change, and the symbolism of fashion changes too. Some Christian colleges still ban beards on their students' and faculties' faces because the schools' administrators came of age in the sixties when beards were often a sign of rebellion. To say that a boy with a pierced ear is promoting a homosexual lifestyle sounds equally absurd. One student's choice of style should never be disrupting to other students' learning, but the standards that schools impose about clothing and grooming need to be justified realistically. Sometimes a school's rules of dress are simply matters of taste. That's okay, but a school should be willing to admit it when this is the case rather than trying to justify every aspect of the student dress code as being "biblical." Such contrivances do not fool students and generally do more harm than good.

This is not to say that clothing doesn't have an impact on the real, day-to-day dynamics of a school. Studies show that students who dress conscientiously for school tend to take their studies more seriously and to perform better. The goals of any dress code ought to be to reduce the stress that kids (and their parents!) face with clothing choices, to present students as serious about the task of learning and respectful of the privilege to learn, and to anticipate the professional decorum that will be required of most of our students at some point in their future.

Another category of student deportment is social manners. Students who speak respectfully to adults, who talk to one another in mannerly terms, and who follow general expectations of social etiquette benefit the school in a number of ways. First, they reflect proper Christian submission by interacting with adults in ways that recognize the divinely ordained authority of teachers, administrators, and coaches. Though we live in a democratic society, the universe is hierarchical, and God has designed people to live prosperously under the authority of others. Recognizing this principle is a step toward Christian maturity that cannot be skipped.

Second, well-mannered students promote the harmony that ought to characterize a community that has committed itself to the biblical notion of *mutual* submission. This sense of harmony and cooperation is evidenced when people open doors for one another, allow others to move ahead in lines, or put someone else's interests before their own.

Third, students who habitually treat others respectfully reflect well on the school. Parents, grandparents, and anyone else associated with a school are glad and impressed with the seriousness of the school's mission when it is reflected in kids who know how to behave themselves. It is not hypocritical to ask children to behave for just this reason. Every student and every teacher is an ambassador of the school's mission. The goal of everyone ought to be, at the least, not to give an outsider reason to doubt the sincerity or the success of the school and the people who learn and work there every day.

PROFESSIONAL COMPORTMENT

Faculty and staff are not immune from the need to reflect well on the school and to promote its cultural values in obvious ways. At Our Savior Lutheran School in Houston, Texas, students wear uniforms to school, and so do teachers. Faculty polo shirts embroidered with the school's crest communicate that they are proud to be teachers in this school, teaching these students. Short of a faculty uniform, teachers and others who work in a Christian school need to dress as if they are going to work. Teachers in some public school districts have made a mockery of faculty dress standards, resulting in buildings filled with teachers who look as if they just rolled out of bed. Not only does sloppy dress demean the profession, it also demeans students who know when someone did or did not put an effort into showing up for work today.

Faculty should, of course, not only dress professionally, but also behave professionally. We have already addressed matters of mutual respect and courtesy, but these extend particularly to the sadly common matters of gossip, breaches of confidentiality, politicking, shortcutting procedures, showing up late, missing meetings, leaving meetings to take cell phone calls, etc. All these habits corrode a school's effectiveness.

CLASSROOM MANAGEMENT

One of the most important impressions anyone can get of a school is the first impression upon entering any classroom. Are students busy? Is the teacher in control? Do students seem energetic? Is there a sense of purposefulness in the room? Does everyone seem relaxed? Is there constructive conversation? Are ordinary problems solved in an ordinary fashion? Is any joy evident?

A teacher's ability to manage a classroom has to do with a lot more than staying on task, keeping order, and getting through the curriculum. Managing a classroom is really a matter of guiding the personalities in the classroom. Each student brings a different set of needs, motivations, expectations, and skills. Directing this immense psychological combination over the course of thirty-odd weeks, accomplishing important tasks, and leading students toward friendships that may last a lifetime is an extraordinary and demanding responsibility.

Many of the problems teachers face in class are a simple matter of arrangement. I (Littlejohn) have long said I could tell who does the teaching as soon as I walk into a class. If desks are arranged in pods of four with students facing each other, requiring them to look right, left, or behind them to find the teacher or the board, then students are learning from each other and on their own. If desks are arranged facing the front, then students are learning from the teacher. This may seem an oversimplification, but in the lower grades when students learn didactically by "direct instruction" we expect teachers to teach, and students will be less distracted if they are directed toward the center of learning. Of course as students mature, we want them to be taught Socratically. Many upper-school classrooms should be arranged in circles or horseshoes in reflection of this pedagogical method.

In any case, the key to managing a classroom well is balance. As the passage from Ecclesiastes says, there is a time for everything. A time to work and a time to play. A time to be silly and a time to be serious. A time to be quiet and a time to shout. A time to feel bad and a time to celebrate. The skilled teacher balances all of this, keeping his or her eye on the school's mission and culture, while investing all of the necessary energy into the classroom and the students who inhabit it with him or her.

CLASS SIZE

Among the factors that contribute to a teacher's ability to effectively manage his or her class is class size. In recent years, this topic has been the center of considerable attention, controversy, and political action, but the research conducted over the past two decades on the issue has been completely inconclusive. In the first place, published studies of class size to date have focused on the public school environment, and none of the studies have been sufficiently controlled to isolate the effects of this single variable.

We are aware of no study that has demonstrated changes in student performance with incremental changes in class size (e.g., at what number of students class performance on standardized tests makes a significant shift), but reports have generally concluded that student performance is better in "small" classes than in "large." The problem has been in the identification of what constitutes large versus small. Some studies have compared classes of thirty-five to classes of seventeen, while others have compared classes of twenty-eight to classes of thirteen.

What has been evident from the existing studies is that statistically significant learning improvements were observed among students from low socioeconomic, minority, ESL, and "absent parent" backgrounds and among those with identifiable learning difficulties in small versus large classes, while little to no difference has been observed among other students. These findings would suggest what intuition and experience have long told us—that other factors contribute to student learning, irrespective of class size. Among these factors are parental involvement and support, student facility with the English language, and a teacher's ability to devote individual attention to students with special learning needs.

Interestingly, studies that considered the combined effects of special teacher training together with assignments in smaller classes observed no change in teaching methodology employed by teachers despite their training. We are not sure what to make of these observations, but we have long maintained that an ill-prepared or unmotivated teacher can no more effectively teach a class of three than a class of thirty.

Determining class size, then, must take many factors into consideration. How prepared are our teachers to engage their students in the liberal arts approach? How motivated are our teachers? How engaged are parents in their child's learning process? How effective has our admissions process been in properly placing students? And how equipped are teachers to manage the special needs of certain students without neglecting the needs of others? These considerations suggest that class size may need to be determined individually (i.e., class by class) rather than universally.

Contrary to conventional wisdom, we would also suggest that the didactic, direct instruction that we propose in the lower grades lends itself to larger classes, while the Socratic methodologies we recommend for older students are better achieved in smaller classes. While we are in no better position than others to suggest a "cut-off" point for any particular grade, our experience at least tells us that the methods we embrace have proven effective with lower school classes as large as twenty-four and with upper school classes as large as twenty.

Even these numbers may be difficult to defend before those who have heard of or have been part of the public school class size debates or who are used to independent school norms. There are certainly financial implications for whatever a school determines is its ideal class size. Class sizes should suit the age of the students and the learning activities that will engage them. And class sizes should fit within the context of a school's pricing and enrollment management plans. Hard and fast policies should be carefully considered, as the law of unintended consequences often lurks behind these types of challenging decisions.

PHYSICAL IMAGERY

Each year I (Evans) return with my family to Ocean City, New Jersey, for a summer vacation. This year, on the way to the boardwalk, we drove by the brand-new Ocean City High School. It occupies a full city block, a stunning piece of classic, brick architecture, complete with columns and arches. The immediate thought came into my head, *These people really care about their high school!* Without knowing one thing about the quality of the school or the commitment of the people who teach and learn there, the beauty of the building itself communicates value.

The liberal arts tradition points us back to truth, goodness, and beauty as foundational values in every person's education. The physical environments of our schools are a prime opportunity to teach our students that beauty is something that God values and that ought to characterize all of our lives.

Yes, we know, we've heard it before, and both authors have said it at some point: "But beautiful buildings cost so much more money!" The simple reply is: "Then wait until you have more money to build." Meanwhile, make sure that the buildings and classrooms you currently occupy are decorated with reproductions of classic works of art and photographs of beautiful things and places, not just cartoon characters. If walls need to be painted, paint them. If the church from which the school is renting space will allow a mural to be painted on a wall, paint it. There is no excuse for schools that purport to teach the absolute values of truth, goodness, and beauty not to make their students' surroundings beautiful.

A biblical principle found in Deuteronomy 4 is worth exploring here. I (Littlejohn) still remember, after nearly four decades, the simple hand-painted placards that hung in the dining hall of the summer camp I attended as a boy: "God First, Others Second, I Am Third" and "Don't Wait to Be a Great Man. Be a Great Boy" (the feminine form of this was displayed during Girls' Camp). There is no question that this three-times-daily reminder for five weeks each summer made a deep impression and, no doubt, contributed to my own early character development. Without overdoing it, we will serve our students well to display carefully chosen, tastefully crafted Scriptures, short poems, and other sayings among the reproductions of fine art, sculpture, and architectural displays that decorate our schools.

ADMISSIONS

Among the greatest influencers of the character of our schools are the standards by which we admit students. Applicants should, of course, be tested for proper academic placement, but the interview with parent and child is equally important. How does the family relate to one another? Are there indications of behavioral or relational problems that may disrupt the school's environment?

Our experience has taught us that the real issue in admissions is not whether families personally confess what a Christian liberal arts school confesses, but whether they understand and want the benefits of this education for their children. This is the heart of the idea of "like-mindedness" in a school and is among the things that distinguish schools from families and churches. When faced with a doctrinal statement, many people we have known will sign the agreement, whether they understand what they are being asked to sign or not. If the goal of the admissions process of a school is to gauge like-mindedness, and thereby help ensure that each family will faithfully support the mission of the school, asking people to sign statements or even to read books is not the best approach.

The best test of like-mindedness is a parent's or an older student's ability to talk about the ways in which the education that your school offers will shape the applicant. If the things that a dad says he hopes your school can do for his child reflect the school's mission, then you have a like-minded family. If a family's expectations for the outcome of their children's education are different from or merely tangential to the school's mission, look more closely. Doctrinal agreement may be a useful starting point, but it is no guarantee that any family will allow your teachers to influence their students in the ways that the school has said are most important.

After all, Christian education is not just useful for Christians, just as Christian business ethics are not just useful to Christian shop owners. If the extent of the gospel's benefits were only personal salvation and morality, there would be little reason to think that anyone other than a person who has already put his faith in Christ might be educable. But the message of the gospel is the herald of a civilization with its foundations in heaven, ruled by Christ, and extending over all of the earth. Children whose families may not confess Christ can and should still be educated in the Christian liberal arts and sciences, so that they may come to understand the truth of the Scriptures and the beauty and ordered goodness of nature and human history.

Though we believe that the true knowledge of God and his ways is only accessible through faith, God's grace and mercy extend to all in some way (by God's common grace). Those who do not express personal faith in Christ are still able to reap the communal benefits of the gospel. When a school provides Christian education to non-Christian students and their families, it extends the influence of the gospel not only over individual souls but also over the culture generally. Schools that follow such admissions principles should, of course, seek balance, because the students we admit are significant contributors to our developing school culture.

A related question is, for what kind of student is a liberal arts education designed? Our answer is simple: virtually any and all. We agree with Robert Maynard Hutchins, the legendary president of the University of Chicago, who said, "The best education for the best is the best education for all." How our graduates put their education to work is their affair. Most will continue their education through university and graduate or professional studies. But some will elect to enter a vocation or perhaps the military directly. Whatever their choice, the education is the same: preparation for life! The liberal arts and sciences do not discriminate on the basis of race, gender, socioeconomic background, ethnic origin, or creed. Schools that take necessary measures to ensure a healthy diversity (by this we mean building need-based financial assistance into the annual budget) in their student populations will enrich all their students' learning experience while serving the greater societal need.

Another question for a school to ask is, "For what range of student aptitude will we provide this education?" This is merely a practical question, and the answer is found in any school's willingness and ability to provide resources that permit access to the riches of the tradition for a wide range of student profiles. While the needs of profoundly retarded children are considered differently, the curriculum and pedagogical methods we will propose shortly have long proven successful in imparting wisdom and eloquence to students with diverse learning styles and even to those with certain learning difficulties.

At Veritas Christian Academy near Asheville, North Carolina, the liberal arts program has been adapted for high-functioning autistic students and students with Asperger's syndrome. Veritas staff envisioned the "school within a school" concept when a board member's child was diagnosed with autism. The family needed special resources, but they wanted a liberal arts core curriculum. Qualifying students' overall aptitudes are excellent, but their social and learning needs are far enough beyond the mainstream of student profiles that they warrant a different approach to being taught and assessed. With a high degree of personal attention from well-trained teachers, these students can accomplish most of what their conventionally gifted classmates can achieve, and they have the opportunity to apply their own extraordinary gifts to the liberal arts environment in ways that other students never could.

The key, as the quote from Hutchins implies, is the adherence to a common standard of achievement that requires students to become increasingly conversant within the liberal arts tradition and independently responsible for their own learning. Being able to educate different kinds of students to the standard, whether they have learning disabilities or not, is one of the joys of teaching in a Christian school oriented to the liberal arts.

A word of caution here, though: Schools should be careful not to create inequitable academic environments by including students for whose academic needs the faculty and programs are not equipped. Magnanimous gestures of inclusion can harm a student profoundly if the school cannot provide the support the student needs to rise to the standards that the school has set.

PLANNING

There is no hope for any school to craft the kind of community of faith and learning that we advocate, no possibility of achieving an ethos that intrinsically connotes truth, goodness, and beauty, without being purposeful and strategic about making it happen. It has been said that education lags ten years behind industry and that Christian education lags ten years behind education. This is certainly true when it comes to this topic. It is our solemn assertion that without a carefully crafted strategic planning process, followed by an implementation plan that makes responsibilities clear and specifies indicators of accountability for every person in the organization, there will be no real educational, relational, or organizational quality within the school. Everything from tuition pricing to admissions to teaching third grade geography will be a reflection of the community's commitment (or lack thereof) to these fundamental organizational management issues. To this end, we recommend to our readers Appendix C, where we further address these issues.

five

THE LIBERAL ARTS CURRICULUM

WE UNDERSTAND THE liberal arts approach to quality education to be primarily a worldview, a mind-set, and an ethos that demands careful attention to an inherited body of knowledge and to effective pedagogy more than it insists on adoption of certain published curricula. However, our combined experience has led us to certain observations about curriculum, and we think it valuable to pass these observations along to our readers with the caveat that they not be taken as gospel. Despite the following suggestions, we strongly believe that each school must find its own expression of the liberal arts paradigm and develop and hold to its own *distinctives* while not neglecting the essentials of the approach.

This being said, we wish to affirm to our readers that our view of curriculum is total. If we compare a school to a living organism, the formal curriculum is its skeleton. Curriculum provides both form and the capacity for function. The success of a school's purpose statement is ultimately embodied in the classroom activities and the long-term effect that those activities have on the students' minds and characters and on the shape of their lives. A firm, well-articulated curriculum can allow for a multitude of activities and perspectives within the school while still moving everyone within the community toward common goals.

Because of the varieties of personalities, perspectives, and activities within any school, a well-devised curriculum, like a skeleton, must be both rigid and flexible at the appropriate points. As we have repeated throughout this book, the desired ends will determine the architecture of your school's curriculum.

The first thing to keep in mind is that some aspects of a school's curriculum will always seem to be changing, because the details of how curriculum works often depend upon the personalities who are making it work. Teachers with varying gifts, interests, and backgrounds and students with varying motivations and aptitudes force a state of constant change upon any instructional plan. But just because some things constantly fluctuate doesn't mean that everything must.

The academic plan, as is true for all other expressions of the community of faith and learning, derives from the strategic objectives that result from the strategic planning process. These objectives are nonnegotiable, and they will inform the goals that each school must define for its students. From those goals we must derive those curriculum objectives that are likely to shape our students into the kind of people of whom we will be proud to say, "They were educated in our school."

A curriculum objective is essentially a desired outcome from some set of organized activities. In order for it to guide our work, an objective must be achievable (that is, it is possible, given what we know about human nature, the condition of our society, the skill of our teachers, the aptitude of our students, etc.) and measurable (that is, it must describe something that can be observed in a student or measured statistically). Honesty is a laudable virtue, but it is an impractical curriculum objective. On the other hand, "That students have learned to discern between true and false statements and can articulate the moral significance of honesty" is a measurable outcome that we have not failed to achieve if one of our seventh graders tells a lie.

Every level of curricular planning should begin with a set of objectives to which the school's programs and activities will answer. Ideally, if you can't justify an activity by its contribution to your school's curriculum objectives, you shouldn't be doing it. Different levels of curricular objectives will require varying degrees of commitment. Typically, published curriculum guides place all curricular commitments at the same level. Either every aspect of the curriculum is indispensable or none of it is. This perspective is both unhealthy and impractical.

Curricular priorities must be set by the school and must be strictly adhered to. If, for example, the fourth grade curriculum has set reading and math as its highest priorities, time spent on these subjects should reflect that priority. Without such clear direction, a teacher who loves history or music will gravitate toward spending more time on these than on math and risks failing to help her students achieve sufficient mastery of the subject to matriculate to fifth grade. A valuable exercise for teachers is to track periodically the minutes spent on each subject for a week as a self-measure of staying the course with respect to curricular priorities. At the same time, it is important not to assume that time on task is the only indicator of curricular priorities. The best measure is whether sufficient time has been provided for students to master the skill or content in question, but twenty minutes on a subject that deserves two hours indicates insufficient prioritization.

In designing or revising curriculum, then, we suggest that you begin with the "non-negotiables." These are the goals on which you will not negotiate with "curriculum terrorists." Every school has these well-intentioned individuals. Sometimes they are parents or board members who envision themselves as "agents of change." Sometimes they are faculty members who don't want to adjust their thinking to the school's priorities. The point is that every school needs to know what its non-negotiable objectives are when it comes to the experience of each student—and the list should be kept relatively short.

From these overarching, non-negotiable objectives, we define instructional principles that describe the *environment* in which we will seek to achieve our larger goals. For example, how will we approach the need to build a base of foundational knowledge for each discipline in the grammar school? How will we address the differences in cognitive and social development that become evident between boys and girls in the middle years? How will we structure our courses to emphasize mastery and avoid unhelpful redundancy in the upper school? Answers to these types of questions help specify our approach to solving problems that every school encounters, and they give faculty, students, and parents a clearer picture of our educational values.

Instructional principles inform the goals we set for each discipline at the grade level, and these grade-level goals guide the syllabi and lesson plans that the faculty develops to achieve the goals. We recommend that administrators exercise less control over the methods that are used to achieve the school's educational objectives the closer the plans get to the students' actual daily experience. A school with dependable hiring practices and clearly articulated objectives should be able to depend on its teachers to create and coordinate the various methods, or range of methods, that will be necessary to help each child achieve what she can in the context of the school's mission. Accountability and room for creativity are the outcomes that should emerge from a solid curriculum planning process.

Let us make one more point here: curriculum plans do not begin with a way to teach something. If we accept Dorothy Sayers's suggestions regarding the "lost tools of learning" without examining the ancient and medieval methods she heralds, we might conclude that liberal arts learning concentrates almost entirely on pedagogy and cares little for curricular content. On the contrary, the tradition handed us by our forebears says little to nothing about pedagogy, while saying everything about curriculum. The *trivium* is not a pedagogical paradigm, but a collection of disciplines, the study of which imparts a set of linguistic skills and knowledge that are transferable to other subjects. From Pythagoras to Augustine to Hugo of St. Victor, the evolution of the liberal arts has been about curriculum, curriculum, and curriculum! Curricular plans begin with goals, and the more achievable and measurable the goals, the better the plan will be.

THE 12-K CURRICULUM

Over the past decade or more, there has been a proliferation of new school growth in America. The "classical and Christian" school movement, public charter schools, individualized instruction programs for students with learning differences and disabilities, and "university" model homeschooling programs have all contributed to the range of options that parents have for educating their children. Many of these schools have been founded by parents of school-aged children for their own children and their friends' children. The one thing that each of these parent-initiated schools has in common is the need to plan a curriculum—and the options can seem endless.

Established schools have their own curriculum structures to which they must answer, and faculty, students, and parents all have a crucial stake in the integrity and predictability of what they encounter in the academic program. In a healthy school, intent on improving the quality of instruction and learning, the curriculum is always under some degree of revision, but typically this revision is at a departmental or grade level, executed primarily by faculty. Wholesale adoption of new paradigms or purposes for the school's curriculum such as we are suggesting should be carefully planned and, as with strategic planning, should include the perspectives of as many categories of stakeholders as possible. Too many school heads or curriculum directors have lost the confidence of their schools by mismanaging change in the academic program.

Whether you are working to get a program growing or improving the purposefulness of an existing program, meaningful curriculum planning must begin with the end firmly in mind. Most curriculum planning processes start at the bottom and work up in a building-block fashion. "Let's decide what our kindergarten program should look like, then first grade, etc." The inevitable result of this kind of planning is that a good deal of the curriculum's objectives will occur accidentally or will mimic the personal experiences of those who are designing the curriculum. The only type of grade-to-grade coordination the building-block approach permits is what we call "picking up where we left off"—that is, sixth grade begins where fifth grade left off, instead of fifth grade ending where sixth grade needs to begin.

The better approach to curriculum design begins with the ultimate or strategic objectives for each student in view, then describes and defines measurable indicators of the successful completion of those objectives at the highest point in the curriculum. If the school ends at twelfth grade, start there; if eighth or fifth, then start planning there. Defining the end result of the education that we wish to provide produces a downward pressure on each grade beneath and plans answers for the goals, rather than the goals being defined by how much a class or teacher could accomplish in any given year.

Let's use a history program as a brief example. If the larger objective of the history curriculum is for students "to have gained a grasp of the expanse of Western civilization and its crucial interactions with the rest of the world through the current generation," where must the planning start? With "the current generation," the identified end of the instructional process. Each historical period must be blocked out from the standpoint of time commitment, and the events of each period must be prioritized according to their relevance to the goals and to the intended effect of the total program.

To lend clarity to the prioritization process, we begin by asking and answering the question, "What effect do we wish our history program to have had on our seniors (or eighth graders) by the time they graduate, and how will we measure that effect?" This question does several things for us. First, it focuses our attention on our students, keeping the benefits to them in the forefront of our considerations. Second, it forces us to plan 12-K rather than the less effective reverse process. Third, it leads us beyond goals that can be defined merely academically; that is, it compels us to examine the effect upon the whole student including the information he'll gain, the attitudes and motivations he'll demonstrate, the degree to which he integrates historical perspectives into his own worldview, etc. And, fourth, it forces the conversation toward concrete indicators of success or failure instead of settling for vague, subjective outcomes.

This is difficult work, and many teachers would rather just jump to the "what are we going to do?" questions, but the benefits of 12-K planning to a sense of coordination and ease of future planning are incalculable. Whether planning a brand-new program or revising an existing one, then, we recommend the same process. Write the curriculum from the top down rather than from the bottom up in order to gain a more purposeful, coordinated understanding of the whole program.

DESIGNING THE CURRICULAR SCOPE AND SEQUENCE

Let us now describe the process in greater detail. There is no way to accomplish an all-encompassing, top-down, 12-K scope and sequence without assembling the key stakeholders for a working summit on curriculum design. In fact, practically speaking, it may take several such summits to accomplish the task. After all, we are not relinquishing the educational destinies of our students to university curriculum designers (Christian or otherwise) or to the textbook publishers (Christian or otherwise). Such "boxed" curricula may make life easy for teachers by relieving them of the necessity to think, but none to date addresses the instructional essentials of a liberal arts paradigm. Even if they did, an unexamined adoption of such a curriculum would be antithetical to the kind of teaching and learning we so highly value.

Ideally, such summits would be scheduled beginning in the early spring semester, should involve all faculty and academic administrators, and should be open to board members and parents who are sufficiently interested and willing to commit to participating at all summits. Unless a distraction-free focus can be ensured on campus, an off-site meeting facility should be arranged. A three-day summer summit may suffice for our purposes, but this is hard work and may be best tackled in shorter, one-day bursts in order to avoid burnout and the accompanying tapering off of quality toward the end of the process.

With everyone present, the school's strategic objectives should be rehearsed and the questions answered: "What are the major skills, knowledge, and virtues we want manifested in each of our graduates?" "Are they achievable, and how will we measure them?" Of course, we are suggesting that wisdom and eloquence embody the essence of what we ultimately wish to impart to our students, but what specific skills, knowledge, and virtues will our wise and eloquent graduates possess? Although this may be accomplished internally, a facilitated Appreciative Inquiry[1] process may well serve this phase of academic planning. Next, the specific outcomes for the various disciplines taught should be determined in small groups: the fine arts faculty, the math faculty, the science faculty, the history faculty, the English faculty, the foreign language faculty, the Bible faculty. These meetings should take place in groups with elementary faculty, administrators, and parents joining in with the disciplines about which they are most passionate. Smaller schools will combine disciplines as necessary (e.g., math and science, social sciences, etc.).

At the risk of seeming self-serving, the authors suggest that group discussions begin by referring to the pertinent section from the ensuing chapters on the disciplines and to the general curricular principles that immediately follow this section. The specific work of determining the outcomes for each grade level then begins: after the desired outcomes are determined for our graduates, we determine them for eleventh grade, then tenth, and on down to kindergarten. As we will see shortly, it may be prudent to work the upper grades in clusters (e.g., 10-12 and 7-9) since students will likely be grouped according to ability and preparation rather than by strict age/grade level.

Since elementary teachers are responsible for a variety of disciplines, once the upper school outcomes have been identified, the elementary teachers will need to work as a group to establish the scope and sequence for all the subjects. From the work already done, the upper school faculty can begin writing syllabi for each course taught. Schools should have a standard form for all syllabi that addresses specific learning objectives to be accomplished, materials to be used, learning activities, and assessment means. For the liberal arts curriculum, the syllabus should also address the integration of faith and learning and the integration of each discipline with the others, particularly the role of dialectic and rhetoric in each course. This is to say that the upper school should have both a comprehensive scope and sequence and, for each course, a syllabus. Both should be made public, available in paper form and, when possible, on the school's web site. If properly done, these documents will prove an effective recruiting and marketing tool.

GENERAL PRINCIPLES

General principles are necessary before we move on to selecting instructional materials and to finalizing the elementary scope and sequence. First, every discipline should be taught from the perspective of practitioners of that discipline, as well as in ways that transcend the thinking of practitioners by applying skills and knowledge derived from each discipline to the other. For example, many science text series approach the subject as if it were history or literature with no emphasis upon the experimental and natural history dimensions of the discipline. Science should be taught as science, and students, when learning science, should learn to think about science as scientists do. And they should "do" science through conducting experiments and gathering data from these experiments and from nature that can then be analyzed, synthesized, and summarized into conclusive reports on the topic. This provides a great opportunity to develop and exercise both mathematical and dialectical skills and even rudimentary rhetorical skills. It also provides an opportunity to transfer the learned principles of objectivity and repeatability to other disciplines such as biblical interpretation or literary criticism. Likewise, students should learn to "do" and think about music, foreign language, history, and tennis (to name a few) like practitioners of these disciplines.

Second, a cyclical treatment of the subjects through the elementary years will accomplish sound principles of teaching and learning. In unstructured or text-directed curricula, there is a tendency to revisit certain topics every year according to the teacher's interest while other important topics are completely neglected throughout the student's entire educational career. The most common example of this is the ubiquitous redundancy of the annual unit on the American Indian at Thanksgiving. While it is important for each student to have exposure to the historic and cultural significance of Native Americans, it is counterproductive to repeat the lesson every year. However, since "repetition is the mother of learning" but redundancy is to be avoided, a carefully planned cycle of coverage in all the disciplines, increasing the depth of understanding of the subject with each cycle, is ideal. For example, if the upper school Bible faculty indicate the need for every student to have a working knowledge of the Old and New Testaments by the time they reach ninth grade, a three-year repeating cycle of Old and New Testament lessons K-2, 3-5, and 6-8 will do nicely. With each cycle, students gain a deeper understanding of the subject while drawing upon things remembered from the previous cycle. In this way, students gain age-appropriate exposure and familiarity with the subject matter while looking forward to addressing it again in greater depth three years up the road.

For those disciplines that rely heavily on acquiring a cumulative knowledge of the subject, like math or foreign language, review and repetition will be on a short and regular (perhaps weekly or monthly) cycle. But three-year cycling is appropriate for disciplines such as history and science, since we want our students to be exposed to a full complement of the disciplinary subtopics but cannot allow too much time to pass before revisiting any given subtopic.

Third, for each discipline there are foundational elements that, in the liberal arts approach, must be committed to memory early in the students' learning experience. We will offer more specifics about this later, including some theory on helping students to master these rudiments, but identifying them is an important element of the curriculum development process. The essential nature of this practice is that such knowledge gives students a structural framework into which they can fit the whole of each discipline as it unfolds to them throughout their academic careers and through life. We cannot provide an exhaustive list of these elements for each discipline but will offer a few by way of example, believing that this work is best done by qualified faculty in each discipline.

In Bible, this may take the form of committing to memory the books of the Bible in order; in history, rehearsal of key events and dates;[2] in geography, the continents, the nations of the world, the states and capitals, and please include the provinces, states, and capitals of our neighbors Canada and Mexico as well as major geographic formations in North America; in math, the times tables; in Latin and modern foreign language, recitation of verb conjugations and noun declensions; in English grammar, the parts of speech; in music, key composers; in literature, important authors, etc. These bits of knowledge, taught early and rehearsed often, will provide for the student, in each discipline, the facility that the alphabet song provides us all in alphabetizing lists and using a dictionary or encyclopedia.

Fourth, beginning perhaps in the middle years, students should be grouped for certain subjects (those that are either foundational to other learning or that rely heavily on cumulative learning) according to preparation and not according to age. This presents a bit of a scheduling challenge (some might call it a nightmare), but with some creative planning every student can be accommodated. The necessity for this emerges because of students who transfer into the school in later years. The tenth grader who has not taken formal logic will take it with eighth graders (if this is where the curriculum plans it), and incoming students who are deficient in mastery of mathematics will be placed in the appropriate level, albeit with younger students. The same may be true for Latin and rhetoric, etc. At New Covenant Schools in Virginia, continuing juniors and seniors take Koiné (New Testament) Greek (having completed many years of Latin instruction) and advanced rhetoric, while transferring juniors take Latin and logic with younger students. Again, with some creative scheduling every student's needs can be met, but some serious thought must be given to curricular priorities and to what instruction is deemed essential.

This leads us to our fifth (and final) curriculum planning principle. Every school must distinguish between its standard curriculum for continuing students and its graduation requirements. This does not suggest a two-track system, but it does acknowledge that transfer students will often be unable to accomplish the entire curriculum because of time constraints. So, while the standard curriculum includes x years of Latin, y years of logic, z years of rhetoric, etc., how many years of each does the community judge to be required for the stamp of "our graduate" to be proudly bestowed upon a student? These questions will also affect our decision as to how early a student must enroll to be admitted. At New Covenant, we would not accept a transferring student after the third week of class of his or her junior year. From experience we learned that students entering the program after that point simply could not accomplish what we expected of our graduates. It was a real testimony to the rigor and quality of our program that we occasionally had families choose to place their rising senior into our junior class, recognizing that she would not enter college for another two years. At any rate, each school must make these judgments for potential students, and the curriculum (not the school's financial exigency) must determine what is appropriate. The focus must be on the student's academic success and not on concerns like "we really need more boys in our senior class."

FINALIZING THE SCOPE AND SEQUENCE

With these few principles firmly in our grasp, we are ready to select materials and complete our scope and sequence. Again, we recommend against the wholesale adoption of any "canned" curriculum. We believe the use of original materials such as unabridged works by important authors to be invaluable in liberal arts instruction, but we do acknowledge the value in providing teachers and students with textbooks for most subjects. The important thing to remember is that texts should be used as aids in teaching the established curriculum. They are not the curriculum. Teachers should not be tethered to the textbook, and, most important, "getting through the text" is not the major objective. If there is no time for praying mantises, the fact that insects were covered should be sufficient, provided that insects were a learning objective for the year.

In choosing texts and other materials it will be necessary for each school to consider the "bent" that they want in the text. Are our elementary teachers better "Christians" or "scientists"? If the former, we want to choose texts that are strong on science, relying on our teachers to help students think "Christianly" about their science. If the latter, we may need texts strong on "Christian perspective," relying on teachers to fill in the "scientific gaps." As we shall address shortly, all history is written with a bias. For example, some "Christian" history series are decidedly anti-Catholic in perspective, while some secular series are decidedly anti-Christian. In any case, each school must decide what texts will best support their teachers' instruction and the established curriculum objectives.

So, keeping our five principles in the forefront of our thinking, varying texts should be reviewed by a committee of those who will be using them and others to determine which texts best support the intended outcomes of the curriculum. It may be especially important in the elementary and middle grades that the same text series be used throughout or at least through one full cycle of instruction (K-2 or 6-8, for example). It is not necessary that a series address every curricular objective, since it is assumed that other materials will be used for instruction anyway. Then, with texts in hand, the scope and sequence can be finalized. The committee can decide what to use from the texts and what other materials will be required for each cycle and each grade. Again as an example, most science series tackle everything every year— elementary chemistry, elementary geology, animal and plant biology, human biology, etc. The key is to determine on what cycle these will be offered. Might we cover animals and plants in kindergarten and again in third grade and finally in sixth? And how about rocks and the human body in first, fourth, and seventh grades? And so on.

The point is that in every discipline there is too much suggested material to reasonably cover. And in the liberal arts approach, with Latin and logic and rhetoric (oh my!) many teachers and administrators may assume that it will be impossible to accomplish it all. Not so. It is true that there may be many subjects to address, but several factors make it more than feasible. First, there is no compulsion in most states for private schools to cover the traditional "socializing subjects" such as health and sex education. Instead, the astute Christian liberal arts school will provide resources and learning opportunities to parents regarding how to best address such topics with their children in the home environment. But they can be dropped from the curriculum to make room for the essential elements of the curriculum.

Second, it is not necessary that certain essential subjects be taught all year long every year. In fact, we owe it to our students to minimize the number of subjects to which they have to attend during any given grading period. For example, despite our need in the middle grades to address grammar, literature, math, history, science, Bible, Latin, logic, music, art, and theater, we must decide which of these must be taught daily and year-round and which may be taught in "toggling" fashion and alternated by semester or by grading period. Despite the essentiality of both Bible and logic, there is no reason that they cannot be scheduled for the same class period (perhaps, depending on qualifications, even taught by the same teacher) and alternated so that in any given grading period students receive grades for only one of these. In the lower grades, the same may be done for science and history. It all depends on the priorities set by the established curriculum for each discipline in every cycle and grade.

Third, some disciplines may be offered as electives in the same period. Although instruction in music is essential to the liberal arts, a student may have to choose among band, chorus, or individual performance. It may also be that certain essentials must be addressed through required participation in certain after-school activities. This may be a solution to providing consistent instruction and experience in certain of the sports or performing arts, for example. Again, it is up to every school to set its curricular priorities and to become creative, if need be, in fitting it all into the students' learning experience.

ACADEMIC RIGOR

An important dimension in framing the liberal arts and sciences curriculum will be the question of rigor. The essence of Greek education was an extended conversation. Socrates' prototypical approach, engaging students personally and directly regarding the structure of their own thinking, was a common approach to tutoring, and this highly individualized method of instruction takes time. Today's schools cannot afford the luxury of individual instruction, but a great deal of time will still be required of both teacher and student in pursuing the liberal arts approach.

The approach we advocate, in short, is rigorous, and there is no way around that. There is no way to educate a student in this perspective in a small amount of time. But the emphasis of the rigor ought to be on the *quality* of work required of students rather than on *quan-*

tity. It is difficult to prescribe how to accomplish this apart from the context of each school, its culture, and its mission. The ongoing conversation, however, about what this means ought to be taking place in each school, for the sake of the students and their place in the liberal arts tradition.

The heart of the matter is to give students time in increasing measure to reflect carefully on the things they are learning. This means, first and foremost, that out-of-class assignments, regardless of the level, must relate directly to the lessons being covered and that they only be assigned if the same educational benefit cannot be gained without their being assigned. No busywork!

Second, it means allowing students as much in-class or in-school time as possible to begin, if not finish, out-of-class assignments by extending teaching periods to allow for more conversation or for lab activities, for example. It might mean building in study periods to alleviate homework strain for students involved in co-curricular activities. It might mean reducing the number of classes that can meet each week or each quarter to allow more flexibility to the schedule. Developing a schedule for assignments and tests that weighs curricular priorities and student commitments (sport game days, class trips, etc.) is a sure way to optimize time spent on out-of-class work. Perhaps math teachers could give homework on certain days while English homework is given on other days. And tests can be scheduled so as to maximize student performance through ensuring a limited number of assignments on any single day.

Whatever the trade-offs or compromises, a school committed to the liberal arts for its students ought to be able to expect a high level of quality and responsibility from its students without running them into the ground. The key is to have high academic expectations, keep out-of-class assignments "on task," and provide as much time as possible for students to get a jump on assignment completion.

Along these same lines, schools must weigh whether to offer a so-called honors track, especially at the middle and high school levels. While both authors have served schools that have them, and one has been an honors director for a university, we are reticent to offer unqualified support for them for the liberal arts school. Because, as we have previously indicated, a liberal arts education is for everyone, the notion of honors can work against the purpose of providing an education that requires high standards of every student. Nonetheless, we recognize that schools may implement and maintain honors programs for a variety of reasons, not the least of which may be parental demand.

In all events, the critical point to be made is that honors should mean "better," not "harder" or necessarily "more time consuming." If you have a group of students who are faster learners or readers or simply more avid computer users than their peers, take advantage of their abilities by engaging them more deeply in the lessons being learned through additional readings or research assignments. Then use them as a resource in the regular instruction of the class during Socratic discussions and through summarizing things read into salient commentary at appropriate moments in the lesson: "Tom, would you share briefly with the class what you have learned about Octavian's victory over Mark Antony in your reading of the book *Cleopatra* by Michael Grant?" or "Sally, what kinds of interrelations did you discover among the three proteins that form the Pyruvate Dehydrogenase Complex in your research?"

Since writing is always a valuable learning exercise, written summaries of honors readings and research are certainly appropriate, but evaluative assessment can as easily be derived from in-class reporting. The important thing, again, is that honors should be deeper, not harder, and such additional assignments can and should be made for eager students whether honors credit is offered or not.

Finally, what should the school's involvement be with Advanced Placement (AP) course offerings? Again, each school must decide how to address this issue, but integrity in the 12-K scope and sequence should be the highest priority. AP courses, if offered, should be available only in those disciplines in which the curriculum and faculty will produce predictable student success on AP exams.

There are a couple of issues to keep in mind when weighing the appropriateness of AP courses to the curriculum. The first is most central to the exercise of curriculum development. AP programming requires "teaching to the test," which means an authority outside your faculty is determining where you begin your 12-K curricular design. The goals of every AP class cannot align perfectly with the goals of the liberal arts curriculum.

Second, to the extent that AP test goals are not perfectly consistent with the school's curriculum, students will perform accordingly. It is entirely plausible that the very brightest, best-educated student may not do well enough to get college credit for the course. Depending on the program you have put together, this may be a worse reflection on The Educational Testing Service (ETS) than it is on your school, but you can guess who ends up with egg on their face.

Third, a primary driving force for offering AP courses is often that parents demand that their student have the opportunity to gain early college credit. In reality, fewer and fewer universities are granting out-right credit for AP test results, and college faculty are often unimpressed with AP courses. Most selective university departments will have students take their introductory courses anyway, because they want to teach their students the important introductory principles themselves. So, while a student may be granted university "credit" for a class and may be allowed to take Biology 200 (introduction for majors) instead of Biology 101 (introduction for non-majors), he may be unable to apply the AP credit to either the core curriculum requirement or to any major program (i.e., the AP credit may be "wasted"), and the student is assigned to the same course in which he would have been placed anyway. In the end, he may simply graduate with 123 credits (or maybe 140, depending on the number of AP credits earned) when the number to graduate is only 120.

OVERVIEW

From our studies of the historical development of the liberal arts and in recognizing that modern knowledge has, in certain respects, outpaced their canonization, we offer the following summary of the liberal arts (and sciences) for the modern Christian liberal arts school. We recognize that our categorization of certain of the disciplines may seem awkward, but we believe what follows to be a historically credible and practically useful rendering of the arts. Reiterating the importance of designing the curriculum from 12 to K, we have, for reasons of practicality and ease of use for reference purposes, arranged the treatments of the disciplines in the following chapters according to the more customary K-12 arrangement.

THE LIBERAL ARTS AND SCIENCES

The Language Arts (The Trivium Updated)

- Grammar
  - Reading, writing, spelling, and vocabulary
  - English grammar
  - Literature
  - History (historic literature)
  - Foreign and classical language
  - Computer navigation
- Dialectic
  - Logic
  - Debate
  - Civics
- Rhetoric
  - Persuasive speech
  - Composition
  - Theatrical performance
  - Thesis writing and defense

The Mathematical Arts (The Quadrivium Expanded)

- Arithmetic
  - Elementary math through algebra
  - Statistics
  - Calculus
  - Computer science
- Geometry
  - Plane geometry
  - Solid geometry
  - Geography
  - The visual arts (painting, sculpture, architecture)
- Astronomy (expanded to the natural sciences)
  - Geology
  - Physics
  - Chemistry
  - Biology

- Music
  - Theory
  - History
  - Appreciation
  - Performance
  - Dance
  - Sport (gymnasia)

The "True Science"

- Philosophy
- Theology

six

THE LANGUAGE ARTS
(THE *TRIVIUM* UPDATED)

IT IS WORTH REPEATING once more that the *trivium* is not, as some have presumed, a pedagogical method, but a collection of linguistic disciplines that incorporate a particular body of knowledge and whose study imparts a particular set of transferable learning skills. Our view of the modern *trivium* places rhetoric at the apex of knowledge and skills because of our society's posture toward certainty and truth. However, grammar and dialectic are equally essential to our students' gaining facility with language, and the three, when mastered, combine to prepare our young scholars for culture-shaping enterprises.

Grammar is what it seems, even in a modern context: the study of the structure of language. However, from ancient times it has been understood that the effective study of grammar requires both preparation (the development of reading, writing, spelling, and vocabulary skills) and materials for practice (literature, both in the vernacular and in other languages). For the ancients and medieval tutors, most of the available literature had historic, religious, or fanciful emphases. We have included computer navigation, especially keyboarding or touch-typing, if you will, since much of the modern student's interaction will involve the computer and among the skills they master should be a practical facility with that technology. Though the grouping of disciplines, from a modern "silo" perspective, may seem odd, each relates to and is integral to the study of grammar. We have used similar reasoning for our inclusion of the disciplines under dialectic and rhetoric. We begin with grammar.

READING, PENMANSHIP, SPELLING, AND VOCABULARY

There is little question in the mind of astute observers of the history of American educational practice that a marked shift in pedagogy related to reading, writing, and spelling in the 1930s has been the bane of every generation of learners since. With the introduction of Dick and Jane, the *See and Say* method, and Basal Readers, the expectation of the young learner shifted from the practical and "do-able" to the impossible, while the instructional emphasis simultaneously shifted from multi-sensory, multimodal to one that relied almost entirely upon a visual learning modality.

These approaches (the vestiges of which were retained in the so-called *Whole Language* approach) utilized artificial methods of visual association and the reliance on memory to recognize every English word.[1] These methods borrowed, perhaps, the legitimate pedagogy of conversational foreign language instruction to teach English readers to quickly develop a large vocabulary. They used pictures and "sight words" to train children to recognize one word at a time and to recall the physical arrangement of its letters in much the same way as one would recognize the strokes that form a Chinese language character. Basal Readers containing only sight words and illustrative aids accompanied the curriculum. Children were coached through a process of guessing the correct words as teachers or parents helped them surmise the actions that the artist had attempted to depict: Spot running, Dick throwing the ball to Jane, etc.

The unintended and unfortunate effects of the approach were threefold and often imposed a permanent reading and spelling disability on the unsuspecting learner. For example, I (Littlejohn) was recently reminded of a true story of a little girl in the late thirties who spelled the word *lard*, "C-r-i-s-c-o." She picked up on the lettering on the can in the illustration while being coached to say "lard" by her teacher. So much for *See and Say*. Similarly, we mention a reading specialist in appendix A, "A Message to Parents," who could not read Dr. Seuss until graduate school. She could neither decode his nonsensical words nor guess them from his whimsical illustrations. No amount of coaching could help her guess these words. Her only recourse would have been to memorize them all, creating a vocabulary that had no further utility.

More common, perhaps, is my (Littlejohn's) own experience as a middle-aged, highly educated adult who misreads words daily because certain letter combinations trigger a mental image of a certain word that I learned to "see and say" as a child. For example, I may read "incremental" as "incredible" or "residual" as "resistant." You can imagine the difficulty I have as a lay reader when the selected passages are from the Kings or the Chronicles or from some other passage of "begats." I have, of course, developed ways of compensating, but I always read the passages over at home before attempting them publicly at church.

The third unfortunate effect is the alarmingly common occurrence of "creative" or "developmental" spelling (a practice that is widely tolerated by teachers who want their students to be uninhibited in expressing themselves) that results in many educated adults spelling the same word three different ways in the same paragraph. (I am glad to say that I don't suffer from this particular disability. It is a matter of personal pride for me that I misspell words with remarkable consistency. Thank God for "spell check"!)

Despite objections to the contrary, we are not overstating things in identifying these reading and spelling maladies as "disabilities." It is true that they will affect different children (and adults) to differing degrees and also true that some readers have better learned to compensate than have others. Still, they are nonetheless genuine disabilities that, while perhaps exacerbating natural learning difficulties, are themselves acquired (i.e., learned) rather than natural disabilities. They are the result of decades of the *See and Say* method of teaching reading.

How then can children learn the arts of reading, writing, and spelling in ways that result in competency in each? Again, we acknowledge that there are numerous adequate methods, but those that best teach these arts will integrate the three through multi-sensory reinforcement of the rules that govern spelling, penmanship, and phonetic decoding. Instead of memorizing the physical structure of hundreds (and eventually thousands) of English words, students learn the limited number of sounds represented by the letters and letter combinations (seventy or so) that express those sounds in the English language.

There are two ways of doing this. One can learn all the letter combinations that make a particular sound, or one can learn all the sounds that can be made by a particular letter combination. For example, *sh, ch, si, ci* and *ti* can all make the "sh" sound. Alternatively, the letter *a* can be pronounced "ă," "ā," or "ah," and *ch* can "say" "ch," "k," or "sh." Children will learn to read using either approach, and a combination of the two is best. But, since we are teaching the skill of reading and not creative spelling, the latter method is preferred and is the first to teach. If students only learn what letter combinations can make a given sound, (to exaggerate the point) they may spell "fish," g-h-o-t-i, using "gh" as in enough, "o" as in women, and "ti" as in caution.

Despite being hard work, many find that teaching and learning the letters and letter combinations (phonograms) that relate to the familiar vocal sounds (phonemes) is rewarding and even enjoyable for teacher and student alike. The teacher uses flash cards or flip charts of the phonograms and recites the sounds they make in unison with the class while they write each phonogram in their notebooks. The principles of penmanship are taught simultaneously with the sounds of the phonograms. In this way students see, hear, write, and say the sounds, reinforcing their learning through four sensory modes at once.

Once the phonograms are learned, oral recitation of spelling/vocabulary words begins. Students hear the vocabulary word spoken (not written) by the teacher and write it in their notebooks while pronouncing the phonetic sounds they are writing. The teacher coaches the students as to which phonogram is used when multiple options exist (fi*sh* not fi*ti*). Since we will not rely on Basal Readers with their contrived illustrated stories that contain only sight words, spelling and vocabulary can be drawn from lists of words that are most often used or encountered by children in descending order of frequency of use. For example, teachers can employ the sound educational principle of moving incrementally from the familiar to the unfamiliar, rather than drawing vocabulary from groupings of words whose meanings are unrelated such as "Jan, Dan, ran, van, tan, man, can, fan, pan, ban." Such words would doubtless make a lovely story and conjure an imaginative illustration but provide no substitute for the quality literature that children will soon be reading with the integrative method described here.

In our schools in Virginia, every first grader could read by Christmas, but an anecdote from a grateful grandfather is worth recounting here. In January one year this grandfather shared his excitement that, over Christmas break, his first grade granddaughter shocked him by picking up his King James Bible and opening it randomly to Isaiah. As she read a paragraph or more, he recognized that she did not grasp the meaning of what she was reading, but he did! She was decoding the words with such alacrity that he suspected he could not have read the passage any better. This illustrates a point made by Hugo of St. Victor and Dorothy Sayers: developing a skill does not require a full understanding of the material upon which the student is practicing the skill. That understanding will come later, and its facility will be greatly eased by the fact that the mechanics and the meaning do not have to be simultaneously grasped. The mechanics will be second nature (like the mechanics of driving a car) so that the understanding will be easier (like following a map in an unfamiliar city). The one is not hampered by our lack of facility in the other.

It is noteworthy that naming the letters of the alphabet is of little value to the nonreader. Knowing the alphabet, while certainly "elementary," is of greater use in learning the more advanced "numeric" skill of alphabetizing than it is to reading. After all, knowing that *w* is pronounced "double you" is of little value in decoding "cow," which simply employs two sounds: the "k" from the phonogram *c*, which can say "k" or "s" (think sounds, not names) and the most common pronunciation of *ow* which can say "ow" or "oh." A little coaching is required for students to correctly write the oral vocabulary, and the teacher makes the rounds to ensure that everyone is learning properly. Again, four sensory modalities impinge upon the student's learning. As students learn to write the sounds they hear, they soon realize that they can "hear" the sounds they are writing and see on the page. In the short time it takes to learn just seventy phonograms the student has acquired the ability to decode (i.e., read) any English word she encounters.

As students advance in their reading skills and make their way through the spelling/vocabulary lists to more advanced words, the spelling rules are reinforced with every new word. Did we say "rules"? Yes, like you, we remember only one from our own schooling: "*i* before *e* except after *c*." Some remember the longer version: "or when sounded as *a* as in neighbor and weigh."

But other principles of spelling can be broadly applied and ensure that students don't suffer from the poor spelling habits of previous generations. For example, "English words never end in *v*, *i*, or *u* except for

93

the word you" (*ski* is a French word we have borrowed along with the enjoyable activity it names). So in spelling the word *have*, for example, a student must add a silent *e* (since "English words never end in *v*, *i*, or *u*") and rehearse at the time which of the five kinds of silent *e*'s they have used. Students also learn which of the five forms of "ir" to use in spelling (*er*, *ir*, *ur*, *or*, and *ear*), and about forty-five other rules of spelling are reviewed as they apply to the introduction of each new word affected by the rule. Parents may at first resist the regular testing of thirty spelling/vocabulary words in first grade each week (six new words daily) but will soon see the power of this approach in their children's facility for reading and spelling.

Frankly, nothing in all of education is more satisfying than helping nonreaders become readers and opening for them the doors to the literary and cultural treasures contained in our language. The fascinating thing is that the integrative method we have described works equally well for children and adults and with those for whom English is a second language. And with patience, it even works for those with certain learning disabilities. In fact, by now some may recognize from this description the methodology developed by neuroscientists Orton and Guillingham[2] for use with children with learning disabilities. It is the method that the visiting reading specialist in appendix A (who could not read Dr. Seuss) was delighted to find successful for whole classes of traditional learners, as well as for the individual tutoring of "special" students.

Reading mastery is foundational to our learning. Yet many of our students will transfer in from other schools, having missed the benefits of such a program. So it is essential for such students and is necessary as reinforcement for returning students for each grade, at least through sixth, to review the skills and rules of the method at the beginning of each year.

Sixth graders may review in two weeks what first graders cover in a year and what third graders address in six weeks, but such review is essential to the students' ability to move forward with vocabulary, spelling, and even reading. Despite the departure from modern conventional wisdom, teachers will find that this is time well spent. In some, if not many, cases with transferring students, requiring them to complete a summer term to gain sufficient facility in these skills before joining in with their new fellows may be needed. Students who have particular difficulty because of a second language or learning challenges may well benefit from a regular after-school tutoring regimen to help them keep pace with their classmates.

ENGLISH GRAMMAR

While modern education has gradually postponed the learning of English grammar, including the parts of speech and good old-fashioned sentence diagramming, from elementary to middle to high school, a liberal arts curriculum demands that grammar be taught soon after children learn to read (e.g., beginning in January of their first grade year, if not sooner). Indeed, educators from classical Greece through early twentieth-century American schools insisted on grammatical studies as foundational to everything else.

Students should be introduced to the complex structure of language so that their linguistic skills are not handicapped by an inadequate understanding of how we use words to make sense. The rules of language usage and style are essential as students mature in their abilities to read and write. But grammar has fallen out of fashion. In many schools, its formal study has been entirely replaced with inductive composition exercises, requiring only tangential references to the beautiful structures that make the language itself work. The burden, then, falls to us to train a generation of students who know the difference between a gerund and a participle and who understand how language functions so they can be confident in their own artistic use of it.

We are constantly amazed by the ability of our students who have just learned to read to recite parts of speech and to begin to analyze syntax. It should seem self-evident that understanding the structure of something makes it easier to use. To take our previous illustration a bit further, a race car driver who does not understand how his car works cannot advise his mechanics on how the car is performing. And a student who does not understand grammar cannot advise his teacher where he is struggling with his composition. The earlier that a student begins to learn the structure of language, the greater facility he will gain with language over time. As students begin acquiring dialectical and rhetorical skills, they will benefit from deeper analysis of grammatical cause and effect and will experiment with grammatical nuance, learning its power as a persuasive and even clever device. As Winston Churchill is said to have quipped, "The improper use of grammar is something up with which we shall not put."

The thorough understanding of grammar also introduces students to more advanced skills, and it can provide a useful base for the study of other, related disciplines. Grammatical analysis is a kind of dialectical skill, and there is much that the elementary student can and should learn. The authors have been particularly impressed with the way that Brenda Shurley, creator of Shurley Grammar, has organized the teaching of these elementary grammar skills in ways that are conducive to further liberal arts study. In her method, children learn to recite the parts of speech and components of sentences and paragraphs from memory. Then they learn incrementally to analyze simple, then complex sentences by means of antiphonal questions and answers in chorus. Given the sentence "Mary had a little lamb," students recite the sentence in unison and then ask and answer, "Who had a little lamb? Mary—subject noun. What is being said about Mary? Had—verb. Had what? Lamb—direct object. What kind of lamb? Little—adjective. A—article adjective period, statement, declarative sentence. Go back to the verb; divide the complete subject from the complete predicate." In this way, students learn in context the parts of speech and principles of grammar as applied to increasingly complex sentences as they advance in their cognitive development.

If you completed your own grade school education within the last thirty years, chances are that you were not taught English grammar in a methodical, thorough manner. You might be one who really didn't learn grammar until you were forced to in order to survive college Spanish or seminary Greek. Rigorous grammatical instruction in English provides a useful context for the study of other languages, and vice versa as we will shortly observe. Though most students learn Latin and Greek in a radically different way from learning spoken languages, it is comforting for a student to understand the necessity of grammar in making sense of foreign words and sentences as they develop translation skills. Having a firm base of grammatical knowledge of one's own language provides even greater advantage in learning to negotiate the complexities of a modern foreign language. In either instance, the relevance of all those English lists and forms is easily made obvious by the alert, grammatically aware or skilled teacher.

LITERATURE

If there is a secret to the success of teaching and learning in the liberal arts tradition, it could be stated as: "Read, read, read, and read some more!" Nothing in human experience has a more powerful effect on our cognitive, cultural, social, spiritual, and epistemological development than diving headlong into the ocean of ideas contained in the world of literature. Herein the student gains exposure to the rich genres of lyric, poetry, and epic, of parable, fable, and myth, of monologue, dialogue, and theatrical play, of homily, epistle, and edict, of history and fiction, and of current event and fantasy (which are sometimes hard to distinguish). Herein is fruit for the picking, ingredients for the delightful exercise of grammatical, dialectical, and rhetorical skills.

Starting at the end, what do we want our students to be able to read with comprehension and skill by the time they exit our doors? In a word, *everything*. Mortimer Adler's 1940s classic *How to Read a Book* provides an excellent description of various genres, from the Bible to physics, with pointers on how to read each. Our students should be similarly prepared to read anything put before them as a direct result of having lots of different kinds of literature—varying along the whole range of degrees of difficulty—placed in front of them by us. They should not have to learn to read again once they've left us for the university or any other pursuit. A basically educated person must be one who can be handed any form of literature, from a book of Germanic fairy tales to a calculus handbook, and know how to attack it and make sense of it.

Teachers should never settle for giving their students the banal pabulum of what passes for children's literature these days, especially when everyone from Madonna to Jay Leno is a "children's author." There is too rich a heritage at our fingertips to squander precious time with anything less except, perhaps, for dialectical exercises in which students analyze and critique, learning to discern the true, the good, and the beautiful by contrasting quality literature with that which is none of these. We cannot say this strongly enough: great readers are made by great books, and a steady diet of books that do not both challenge and stimulate the reader weakens both the student's ability and desire to read.

So, beginning with the end in view, what literature should we choose for our students? What canon of literature do we want our students to master by the time they graduate? In our opinion, the literary foundation of our civilization is formed by the Bible and the five major epics of Homer, Virgil, Dante, and Milton. Most of the wisdom of the liberal arts tradition originates in or is illustrated by these works, with most of the ensuing body of literature building upon them. A student who has carefully read at least all of the narrative portions of the Bible and the five other epics has a very firm hold on becoming a well-educated person. Upon this foundation a cathedral of classic works from every genre can be built. Getting there requires strategic design of the school's canon, backing it down from the senior year to kindergarten.

Be careful not to misunderstand what we are advising on this point. The Bible and the epics are some of the most difficult works to read in all of literature. But the more familiar students are with the stories contained in each and with the importance of those stories to our cultural identity, the easier the transition will be from stories based on the original works or short pieces of reading to the works themselves, when the time is right. We recommend that a school's reading program equip students to be able to read Homer unabridged (in lyrical translation) and under careful instruction by ninth grade at the latest. This is hard work, to teach and to read. Yet, properly taught, the great books are still as capable of capturing the imaginations of fourteen- and fifteen-year-olds as they have been for centuries.

It is important to mitigate the difficulty of reading such lofty stories by the preparation students receive throughout their schooling, so that what others may view as a burden, our students relish and take pride in. The responsibility of teaching students to love reading great works is made simpler if we know in first grade what they must read in order to comprehend Homer or Isaiah by ninth grade. Homer should not be the first difficult work that our ninth grader has ever read, though he may be the most complex poet a student has read to this point. But the student will have read a great deal of the great poets and playwrights and will have committed to memory whole sections of the Bible and other quotable authors of note, such as Shakespeare or T. S.

Eliot. And applying dialectical skills to these authors will help him see that poets have done more through the centuries than wistfully gaze upon bodies (of water and women).

In the grammar school, and even through the middle years, reading should occupy a hefty portion of every school day in three forms: students reading aloud, students reading silently, and teachers reading aloud from substantial works that exceed their students' reading levels by at least two grade levels—sharpening their listening skills, kindling their imaginations, and instilling a deeper love for stories. These exercises are especially important in today's visual-media-obsessed culture. While reading and listening awaken the imagination and stimulate creativity, visual renditions of the same literature can stifle the imagination, because we rely on someone else to translate the written or spoken word into images for us. For this reason, dramatic renditions of great literature should never replace the books themselves. We want our students to feel cheated if they just "wait for the movie version."

This is not to say that there is no value in purposeful and critical interaction with film renditions of great literature. The emotions can be powerfully stirred through the music and scenery a director chooses for the delivery of timeless lines such as Henry's proclamation that *non nobis* and *te deum* be sung in praise to God while the bodies of the vanquished foes still lie warm upon the battlefield in *Henry V*. As one soldier's song is joined by others' until *non nobis* is heralded by the throng, a deep and lasting impression is created. This is good and beautiful and true learning, but it should not preempt students' impressions of the work through reading (or acting) it for themselves.

For the most part, we believe teachers should steer clear of conventional literature textbooks. Anthologies that provide whole or (for very young students only) carefully abridged sections from great works are a treasure that most students will return to now and then for the rest of their lives. As preparation for the challenge of the great books of our tradition, programs like the *Junior Great Books*[3] series provide poetry and prose by substantial modern authors with additional lesson-planning advice and training provided to get middle-years students talking about literature. Likewise the *Great Books* series and other well-edited collegiate anthologies provide a treasure of literary, cultural, and philosophical meat for the upper grades. Some excellent reading lists for younger students are provided in *The Well-Trained Mind*[4] and *The Writing Road to Reading*.[5]

To gauge student progress in comprehending what they read in the elementary years, regular (not frequent, because reading should be a pleasure, not a drudgery) assessments can be designed and administered. Such assessments can use salient selections from quality works and relevant questions that solicit paraphrasing of the passage and analysis of its meaning and moral content. Similar exercises can be devised to assess student listening skills as well, with the teacher reading the passage, then following with relevant questioning. Teachers are not tethered to boxed curriculum for assessing reading and listening comprehension since standard reading levels can be determined for any work of literature by using simple assessment tools. But teachers should understand that the liberal arts student may be considerably ahead of standard levels for both reading and listening.

HISTORY

If curriculum is a skeleton, history is its backbone. The authors believe that history is best taught chronologically. This might seem too obvious to state, but any social studies teacher can tell you that chronology tends to be the last thing that current publishers think of when they design their curricular materials. That history is, in fact, a story seems to have been lost on many. Instead, we are served with "thematic" studies, in which various cultures and civilizations are compared on the basis of social values, almost irrespective of dates and historical context. We recommend that historical studies begin early and that they follow a sensible timeline of persons and events that repeats regularly. Repetition is an important element of the history curriculum, as it enables students to build on the familiarity of key events while learning to investigate with increasing analytical skill.

To build on the example we suggested earlier, planning in the history curriculum is key. As educational administrators, we are frustrated by the common approach to teaching history that makes its goal to "get through the book." The school's curriculum, and not the textbook publisher, should set the goals and priorities for the history program and for each student's experience in it. Not every historical event is equally important, and the historians in the school need to take responsibility for what the curriculum will address and how.

The traditional view of history is that it represents a flow of human political, cultural, social, and moral development, revealing to the analyst a sequence of rational, predictable causes and effects. The Christian view of history is that this flow of human experience is inextricably tied to God's providence.

As is true for all disciplines, our understanding of human history is directly affected by our worldview. If we understand human history to be part of God's general revelation of himself to his image-bearers, complementary to his special revelation in the Scriptures, there is much theology to be learned in the analysis of historical events. To use a trite expression, it is after all "his story," and there is to be seen in the flow of human history an unfolding of truth, goodness, and beauty that can emanate only from the Creator and Guardian of human life. And a student's faith can deepen greatly as he comes to perceive God's hand of providence through the course of human events.

Our job as historians is to reconstruct the events of the past, to analyze them, and, as Christian practitioners of the discipline, to make informed judgments and learn from what has gone on before. Through the progression of reconstruction,[6] analysis, and judgment, our students come to realize that, like those who have gone before, they can be intentional makers and shapers of history and culture.

It has been said many times, "those who are ignorant of history are doomed to repeat it." This points out the heart of the historical enterprise—to gain wisdom. The liberal arts school builds its curricular identity around the study of history, because we are constantly looking for ideas and actions that produced peace and prosperity and that are worth emulating in our own time. The pursuit of wisdom does not just stop with the study of the Scriptures or ancient philosophers. It involves a constant rehearsal of the past to discern who did what, why, and to what effect. This is especially important to the school that is shaping cultural leaders. As we encourage our students to look beyond their own interests to the interests of society and the common good, we want to be sure to have provided them with plenty of historical examples of others who have done the same and have both succeeded and failed.

The ancients viewed history almost entirely through a moral lens.

Sit down with Thucydides or Plutarch or even Josephus, and what one finds are often extended essays on the characters of those who acted most prominently on history's stage. Plutarch is especially useful, as the genre he employs (Praise and Censure) is one of the preliminary exercises to formal rhetoric. In this exercise, the student compares two contemporary characters, the effect they had on the world, and the elements of their moral vision that led to the effects of their leadership. Not only do exercises like this solidify historical facts in students' memories, but they also formalize and deepen the students' ability to look at historical events and characters methodically and consistently. While this is not a commonly accepted approach to modern historical studies, the knowledge that students with this kind of analytical background bring to their collegiate studies distinguishes them as being thoughtful and informed.

This may be the best place to remind ourselves to approach our quest for historic truth with our students cautiously. From ancient times, most surviving recorded history has been penned by or at the direction of the powerful and victorious—with the intent of impressing hearers and readers through an exaggerated perspective of that power and victory, often for political purposes. For this reason, students should be taught to read history with a cautious and analytical eye, recognizing the bias inherent in any written record of past events. In this regard, a wonderful dialectic exercise is for students to consider two or more accounts of the same historic event, comparing and contrasting the accounts to glean what truth they may from the record.[7]

Further, a variety of unhelpful, even harmful approaches to the study of history should be avoided with younger children and critiqued by older students. Clearly, tendencies toward naturalistic presuppositions that espouse the inevitable progress of human triumph over all circumstances have no place in the Christian faculty or curriculum except as fodder for dialectic examination. Skeptical views of history that understand events to inevitably cycle meaninglessly back upon one another are equally inappropriate. And blanket assertions of the superiority of one culture or civilization (even our own!) over another, apart from the analytical grid of the culture of the kingdom of God, can produce un-Christian perspectives of ethnocentrism, jingoism, and xenophobia among our students.

Students should be helped to see God's hand in history as transcendent of human plans instead of embracing the simplistic notion that God chooses a "side to back" as if the unfolding of providence were as insignificant as the outcome of a football game. Likewise, the recent cultural struggle resulting in near deification on the one hand and effective demonization on the other of key historic figures is, at best, confusing to students. The biblical treatment of such historic figures as King David or Solomon who, despite their sinful natures and commission of sinful acts, were mightily used by God to further his kingdom on earth provides a more realistic portrayal of human nature and God's grace—and one with which our students are far more likely to identify. Our students should see that the *antithesis* cuts through, not between, people and cultures and the ideas and technologies they have developed. They should also learn that evil can exert short-term triumph over good and that bad things happen to good people, but our just and loving God has a cosmic view of things and is not surprised by the things we struggle to comprehend.

HUMANITIES

It is worth mentioning here that both authors have served schools that combined literature and history in an integrated program called "Humanities." There is much to be gained from a truly integrated curriculum and a double-period offering that effectively ties these two critical disciplines together. One that incorporates Bible and philosophy as well can benefit students and faculty alike.

There are two ways to staff such a course (still others may improve on these two), and each has its strengths and challenges. In one scenario, the same teacher tackles both periods and both (or all) disciplines. Such staffing lends great continuity to the course but may suffer the limitations of a teacher who has training in only one of these disciplines, limiting the insights brought to the table. The other approach assigns a historian and a literature specialist to team-teach the course. If both teachers are "always present," there can be exceptional exchange and growth on the part of both students and faculty. Limiting the time each teacher is in the class will dissipate this benefit accordingly, but committing two teachers to 100 percent involvement can be costly or, if not, can lead to teacher burnout due to too heavy a load. Whether a school uses the humanities approach and whether it includes the "true sciences" of theology and philosophy or whether these disciplines are all separated, the key is to ensure that all objectives for the disciplines included are effectively addressed according to the 12-K academic plan.

CLASSICAL LANGUAGES

There was a time just a generation or so ago that an uncertain college student might decide upon a major in Latin on the premise that "someone will always need a Latin teacher" or that employers recognized that a student of Latin had acquired knowledge and skills easily transferable to a host of business applications. My (Evans's) own father, raised in the working-class suburbs of Boston by Irish immigrants, attended a public high school that required both Latin and the wearing of neckties to school every day. Given today's conventional school curricula and decorum, that seems like another universe altogether.

Happily, Latin has enjoyed something of a comeback recently, even if as an elective discipline. The American Classical League[8] is attracting strong support, most selective universities look favorably upon students with four years of high school Latin, and the AP Latin program remains one of the College Board's most credible courses. During the economic boom of the 1990s, Wall Street firms put out a fresh call for Latin majors to apply because of their reputation as smart, adaptable problem solvers.

The reader may or may not realize that students of Latin often outperform other students on standardized exams like the SAT, but there are more fundamental reasons to require Latin in schools that value the liberal arts tradition. Among them is the *ad fontes* (to the sources) principle from the Renaissance: the ancients are best heard and understood in their own language. In our attempt to recover the benefits of the liberal arts tradition for our children and our culture, it is imperative that we recover the ability to encounter the tradition in its own terms.

But an ironic fate has befallen Latin. Because of its reputation as the "language of scholars," compulsory study has been relegated to the pre-1960s dust heap of "formalism" and "esoterica." Ordinary people are naturally intimidated by people they encounter who have studied Latin or programs of study that require it. What they don't realize is that the "language of scholars" became such because so many people could learn it, providing democratic access to the world of ideas during a time when the globe was hopelessly fractured by vernacular languages and idioms.

No longer a spoken language, Latin is still immensely valuable to those of us who want access for ourselves and for our students to the riches of the liberal arts tradition. To hear Caesar glory in the utility of war or Augustine describe the depth of depravity from which Christ saved him, in their own words, is an extraordinary privilege. And it is a privilege that, pursued in school with sense and purpose, is astonishingly achievable for any student.

Similar thinking applies to the study of Greek and, especially for the budding biblical scholar, the pursuit of Koiné Greek, the language of the New Testament. Despite a plethora of translations, interpretations, and paraphrases available on the market these days, there are many nuances of truths in the Scriptures that evade understanding apart from a knowledge of their original languages. While two years of New Testament Greek by no means makes a scholar, the student who has at least such an introduction to the language will gain a facility in personal Bible study and interpretation that equips him to better apply his dialectical skills to analyzing the commentary and interpretation of the best (and worst) biblical scholars. The challenge, of course, is fitting such study into the already packed curriculum, but the school that values this particular aspect of Christian liberal arts learning will find ways to at least offer Greek as an elective.

There is good reason to teach Latin to younger children (since experience and scientific studies both suggest how much better they are adapted to the skills than are older learners). We acknowledge too that Latin and Greek studies increase a student's facility in English vocabulary and that special skills derive from translating these languages. Yet the trump card in the argument of whether to teach classical languages or not is the language itself and the wealth of cultural revelation recorded therein. The economy, the refinement, the breadth of ideas expressed—these are the essence of the tradition, and they make the study of the language itself indispensable.

MODERN FOREIGN LANGUAGE

A humorous but sad truism about American culture is as follows: "What do you call a person who speaks three languages? Trilingual.

What do you call a person who speaks two languages? Bilingual. And what do you call a person who speaks one language? American." "Many a truth is told in jest," and American education has become the butt of the international community for having neglected the importance of modern foreign language. Ironically, modern foreign language is a curricular point that Dorothy L. Sayers's readers seem to have missed in her writing entirely. Few schools in the classical school movement offer modern foreign language, replacing it entirely with Latin. But for the ancients, Latin and Greek were the vernacular, and facility in both languages was essential to a liberal education. Likewise, the Hebrews (before, during, and after the time of Christ) learned, read, and wrote in Greek (for them a modern foreign language). Sayers herself suggests that such languages should be tackled "along side" Latin.

The benefits are twofold: 1) it gives our students a window into the language and culture of other peoples, perhaps even preparing them to better represent Christ's kingdom to at least one culture besides their own; and 2) it affords them the same great benefit extolled above for Latin, the ability to read certain great authors in their own languages. Whether to teach French (for example) simultaneously with Latin in the grammar school or to have it follow their study of Latin is a matter for the curriculum process, but there is great value in exposing our students to the richness and enjoyment of studying modern foreign language. For some schools (especially those in transition to a liberal arts approach) modern language study may, for some time, be the best and only way to provide the "ancillary" benefits of language study. And in some cases, as it was for The American School of Lyon, France (a classical school for expatriate Anglophones), it may be the permanent choice for obvious reasons.

However, the decision as to which modern foreign language or languages, like all curriculum decisions, must be guided by the intended outcomes and consistent with our overall mission as schools. We are looking for the greatest academic outcomes and not the easy way to socialize or evangelize the nearest growing minority population. It may be socially or economically feasible for northern Minnesotans to learn the Ojibwa language, but what is the academic payoff versus the rich contributions made in other languages? Many factors will influence our choice or choices about modern foreign language instruction, among them the legitimate practical considerations of student/parent demand and teacher availability. But we must also ask ourselves in which languages have the greatest philosophers, historians, scientists, and political strategists handed down their pearls of wisdom and we must weigh all relevant factors in making these important decisions.

COMPUTER NAVIGATION

Computer instruction is the crux of one of the greatest controversies in modern education. Many parents believe that computer skills must be taught in school from the earliest years. School districts spend hundreds of thousands of dollars each year equipping classrooms and labs and replacing equipment that is outdated almost before it is set up and loaded with software. But studies of computer-aided instruction in basic subjects have shown that students learn less and more slowly in the classroom environment when computers are involved. More often than not, computers in the elementary classroom are a distraction that compete for students' attention and draws their focus from the essential instruction of the curriculum. As with the socializing subjects about which we have already spoken, there is no time for computers in the elementary scope and sequence.

However, there is little doubt that students increasingly need to use computers for more than video games and instant messaging. Public and school libraries have long abandoned physical card catalogs in favor of electronic search, and the Internet is providing increasingly reliable materials for legitimate research. What then is the solution for the liberal arts school? We will address the discipline of computer science briefly in the next chapter, but we need here to address the use of the computer as an instrument for gathering and cataloging information, for recording and organizing ideas, and for producing printed reports.

It is a given that students will be using computers for these and other activities, and it is essential that they gain a facility in computer "navigation" that will help them make the best use of their time. Students then should be taught keyboarding or good old-fashioned touch-typing so that each can type from a manuscript or compose at the keyboard using all ten fingers without looking at the keys. A student sufficiently trained in this skill should type 40 to 60 words per minute without errors. Facility in navigating the library resources and the Internet should likewise be taught.

Now here is the controversy: apart from instruction in all aspects of library use by the school librarian, including the electronic search system, the skills just identified, along with facility in word processing and spreadsheet navigation, should be purposefully taught in special classes beginning in the middle years. Some assignments thereafter should purposefully begin to reflect a teacher's expectation that students have acquired these skills. Elementary school assignments, on the other hand, should not reflect such expectations, and students who use the computer at home should not have advantage over those who do not. Superior instruction in the liberal arts does not require the use of computers. Out-of-class assignments should relate strictly to classwork and should be designed to accomplish specific pedagogical aims, neither of which for the grammar school will be computer-related.

DIALECTIC

We use the archaic "dialectic" rather than the more common "logic" to refer to the second liberal art, because of the literal meaning of the words. (We would also suggest that if you mention this art in your school's promotional materials that you also use the word "logic," whatever the esoteric connotation we discuss here.) "Logic," from *logos*, is a broad general reference to good sense, the rational order of things, reason itself. *Dialektike* denotes an artistic skill for which we have natural aptitude but that is not inherent in us at birth—it must be learned. Literally, it is the art of "talking things through."

Perhaps to a greater extent than grammar, dialectic comprises the two complementary elements that define the first three liberal arts: a distinct body of content and a set of transferable skills. Each school that employs the *trivium* must decide the extent to which dialectic occupies the students' time and energy. As with any other pursuit, though, the more you teach, the more confident you can be that the content will achieve priority status in the students' minds.

Crucial to this determination of time spent in the curriculum is to decide ahead of time what needs to be learned and how that content should be demonstrated in transferable skills. We highly recommend that a course in formal logic be included in the curriculum no later than ninth grade and that structured informal instruction in constructing arguments precede this for several years. The formal logic curriculum is important, but there is a very real danger that if broad principles of analysis and argument are not integrated into the students' overall academic habits, much of the logic course is a wasted exercise. Logical thinking, like math computation or essay writing, is a cumulative discipline that cannot be gained in a semester or two.

The goal of studying logic, apart from its inherent cognitive benefits, needs to be articulated and converted into measurable, achievable goals for the classroom environment. Curriculum materials that address "critical thinking" skills for students at various levels of cognitive development are very helpful in developing objectives. A list of types of arguments and fallacies like the sample below, separate from the formal logic curriculum but included in the overall curriculum goals and objectives for a grade or a division, guides the faculty's thinking as they sort through the various available options for emphasis each day in every course they teach.

Sample Goals for Dialectical Instruction Beyond the Formal Curriculum

1. Composing arguments by example.
2. Composing arguments by analogy.
3. Composing arguments from authority.
4. Composing simple syllogisms, proving by deduction.
5. Identifying and avoiding fallacies of conclusions from incomplete information and overgeneralization.
6. Identifying and avoiding fallacies of causation.
7. Memorizing and identifying classical informal fallacies in reasoning.
8. Constructing arguments both in favor of and against the same proposition.

This list is by no means a comprehensive catalog of useful dialectical skills. But it is brief enough to remember and general enough that faculty who lack formal instruction in logic can get started immediately by integrating these types of skills into their courses. Brief, accessible manuals on argumentation and informal logic abound, as college professors have had to respond to the tragic failure of schools to teach students how to think. The constant challenge is to integrate this or some other list into the daily experience of each student in an orderly, predictable way and to be able to assess the progress being made to incorporate these objectives into each discipline.

An interesting dilemma attends our theory of liberal arts learning: The earlier this instruction begins in a student's career, the longer it takes to teach; but the later we wait to begin the instruction, the less time the student has to incorporate each skill as an intellectual habit. Prescribing a dialectical priority in grade school sometimes seems to pit the timing of cognitive development against the need to develop these habits as early as possible. Still, the value is self-evident, and a disciplined effort always pays off in the student's favor.

DEBATE

In addition to logic, or perhaps as part of the formal instruction in logic, students should be introduced to the principles of debate. These skills will doubtless be honed in later years and will intermingle with the study of rhetoric, but their introduction to middle-years students will fall into step with their cognitive and social development (i.e., their natural propensity to be argumentative). As students are learning to reason their way through issues and to construct their thoughts into formal syllogisms, affinity for and pleasure in argumentation develops naturally. Providing such students with rules for civil discourse, whether derived from forensic debate or Lincoln/Douglas-style debate or even from simple principles of courteous classroom discussion, can channel otherwise disruptive energies into valuable learning experiences.

CIVICS

By civics we do not mean political science, with its rehearsal of case law and its effect on political process, but rather the notion of civic responsibility, the dialectical exchange of ideas related to governance of organizations, municipalities, states, and nations—and active participation in the political and electoral processes by the citizens of such institutions. Civics, like debate, is a dialectical discipline but may well be undertaken along with instruction in rhetoric. Like rhetoric, its principles should be introduced very early in the curriculum, but certainly by the middle years. Students should gain a working understanding of constitutions, from that of the local garden club to that of the United States. They should learn to run a meeting according to Robert's Rules of Order and learn the principles necessary to engage respectfully in civil discourse about issues important to society in any forum, from the local barbershop to the Supreme Court.

RHETORIC

Aristotle called rhetoric "the faculty of seeing all the available means of persuasion in any situation,"[9] a set of content and skills with virtually universal relevance and applicability. Rhetoric, we are arguing, is the most powerful element of the *trivium* for the shaping of modern leaders. Rhetorical instruction, however, depends a great deal upon the foundation of grammar and dialectic, which allows for students to gain rapid facility in persuasive discourse. Once a baseline of knowledge and experience is established, we confront the same challenge that we face in dialectical instruction: how to get the discipline to pervade each student's experience.

As with dialectic, we must begin with a clear commitment to teach rhetoric as a discipline (including one to two years of instruction in formal rhetoric) and to integrate clearly articulated skills into our curricular objectives. Here we provide another example of a list of skills that might be used to form the basis for an integrated rhetoric program for middle or upper school students.

Sample Elements of Rhetorical Instruction and Learning

    1. Composing theses/propositions.

    2. Using the common topics in composition.

    3. Researching arguments.

    4. Composing arguments using all three classical modes of appeal.[10]

    5. Composing and arranging *enthymemes*.

    6. Using invalid (yet true!) arguments to persuasive advantage.

    7. Arranging arguments for maximum impact.

    8. Making public, persuasive presentations.

In our chapter on the rhetorical curriculum, we address the complexities and possibilities of teaching for rhetorical effect more comprehensively. The point to be made here is that without a clear sense of the goal in both content and skills, neither can be reckoned on. We will never achieve more than we have carefully and realistically planned to achieve for our students and their education with us.

COMPOSITION, SPEECH MAKING, AND PERFORMANCE

Students should be introduced early to the responsibility of writing, both as a means of creative expression and as the argumentative culmination of good research. Teaching students to write effectively is without doubt a time-consuming responsibility because students are not born with an innate ability for formal writing mechanics. These have to be learned, and the process is pretty much the same for the vast majority of students. Reacting to a student's writing as an editor and allowing for rewritten improvement is the only way to teach this skill. When I (Littlejohn) served as honors director for a major university, I read the honors theses for students from a wide variety of academic departments. On one occasion I encountered a thesis that was utterly incomprehensible and arranged a meeting with the student's departmental advisor. I discovered that the student was a straight-A student, but that the advisor had concerns about his writing similar to my own. As we explored the situation together, we discovered that this student had done well on objective exams and had otherwise sufficiently impressed his professors with his enthusiasm and charisma, so that he always received an A on assigned papers. He had scores of papers with big red A's at the top, but without another single correction or remark to be found on them. His advisor and I agreed with a sense of collegial shame and remorse that most likely no one had ever actually read one of his papers, and now he faced failing his senior thesis because no one had taught him to write.

Despite heavy workloads, it is not sufficient to just *grade* papers. As conscientious teachers in the liberal arts tradition we must *correct* papers. We serve students as editors, respecting their style and voice, but holding them accountable for good grammar, sound logic, and meaningful expression in their writing. It is worth noting, in this context, that a color other than red may prove more encouraging to the young scholar who is struggling to learn the difficult art of effective writing.

A rhetorically oriented school also serves students by helping them get past the fear that plagues a huge majority of American adults: the fear of public speaking. Purposeful composition assignments are an early step toward confidence in front of an audience that can begin in first or second grade. As we teach students to write, we should also teach them the principle that "writing is for reading." Many students approach composition assignments without asking the basic questions, "Who is my audience, and what will they think of my writing?" Having students read their compositions aloud to their peers develops confidence in their writing and gives them practice in basic speech making. As we shall see in an ensuing chapter, the principles of rhetoric can be introduced very early in the curriculum, and everything we do to reinforce the goal of eloquence will pay dividends when our students face real rhetorical challenges.

Among the greatest means to bolster students' rhetorical confidence and to test their writing skill is to require or encourage participation in theatrical performances. Every exposure a student has in the theater, from writing a story based on dialogue, to directing, to playing a leading role, to assisting with costumes or sets strengthens his skill as an eloquent culture shaper.

THESIS WRITING AND DEFENSE

The culmination of a Christian liberal arts education unequivocally should be the selection of a topic, the thorough research of that topic, the composition of a substantial persuasive thesis, and the public oral defense of that thesis before a panel of faculty with peers and parents in attendance. While such a prospect may seem daunting, the liberal arts education experience incrementally building toward this capstone should result in seventeen- and eighteen-year-olds who can confidently and competently perform at this level.

It is not uncommon for schools, especially private schools, to require a senior project that is presented to the student body. Students perform songs that they have written or demonstrate a skill that they've learned or present some other expression of their personalities. These are fine for community building and to celebrate the uniqueness of the students who persevere to graduate from our schools, but the senior rhetorical thesis is something altogether different.

At Regents School, the senior thesis is a full-time required course for each senior, and successful completion of the thesis itself is a requirement for graduation. Early in their senior year, the students begin to explore topics of interest. The criteria are that the thesis must be on a matter of public importance, that it must be controversial, and that it must contain a proposed course of action toward which the speaker seeks to persuade the audience. The students select a faculty advisor who helps to strengthen the research strategy, works with the student to focus the topic, and provides accountability to keep the project on schedule. The faculty advisor will also sit on the six-judge panel when the thesis is presented in the spring.

Meanwhile, students are composing and making speeches on other topics in preparation for the thesis presentation. The rules of presentation are demanding. The speech must be between seventeen and twenty minutes, followed by twenty minutes of questions from the judges. Students are allowed one piece of paper to prompt their memory, but the entire presentation and defense is performed without the aid of any other resource. As intimidating as this sounds, every senior completes the course, demonstrating that the liberal arts tradition really can produce wise and eloquent leaders for our time.

seven

THE MATHEMATICAL ARTS
AND TRUE SCIENCES

AS WE HAVE INDICATED in an earlier chapter, we reject the spurious notion that the *trivium* is foundational to the *quadrivium*. It is certainly true that the classical language arts are foundational to much of learning. It is also true that without the skills that the language arts impart, our student is unlikely to progress very far in any disciplinary pursuit. However, the mathematical arts are, in their own way, equally foundational, and the ancients set for us the example that their instruction should begin at the earliest ages.

The immediate challenge with the mathematical arts, as with all learning, is to make them interesting and enjoyable to the learner. It is a great tragedy in today's educational world that many, if not most, students are turned off to math and science before they have ventured very far into the learning process. And the notion that girls have little aptitude for these arts and should therefore be politely excused from excelling in them is a heretical myth. The more likely cause of student disdain for these arts is the vicious circle that begins with students being ill prepared in these disciplines and then pursuing university teacher education tracks that avoid them, while ultimately being assigned to teach these disciplines in their schools anyway.

It was all too common in our own school experience for the coaches who were hired to build the region's premier athletic programs to be haphazardly assigned to teach biology (perhaps because athletics and biology happen to have the human body as a common focus). Today's approach to handling the high demand and low supply for science teachers is little better, with colleges of education fast-tracking students in "general science education" that typically requires three introductory science courses (e.g., one biology, one chemistry, and one geology) and that's all! Even the finest universities have succumbed to the pressures to water down the disciplinary major or concentration for "the less capable" education student. And colleges of education have become masters ("Aca-magicians," if you will) at outfoxing state legislatures who call for more content in the program by renaming courses and repackaging the same old programs in ways that only an Ed.D. could detect.

Because of the critical importance of the mathematical arts, it is imperative that our schools be diligent in hiring teachers who are both trained in and enthusiastic about them and that we be further diligent in training them to teach these arts effectively. With so many opportunities available in technology-based industries, competent math and science teachers are increasingly hard to find. Christian schools that make scientific understanding a priority may have to reorganize the way teachers are compensated in order to ensure high-quality instruction in these disciplines, but the alternative may be to send students ill prepared into the world.

Careful analysis of math and science curricula should also constitute a high priority. Too often, Christian schools follow one another's curriculum choices without determining the desired outcomes that the curriculum should serve. Every published curriculum program has its drawbacks, and the trade-offs should be identified and carefully considered as instructional materials are chosen. A math program that employs a radical method in the elementary grades may inhibit instruction at the upper levels, when a more conventional approach may be preferred. Conversely, conventional programs are fraught with gaps that undermine the foundations necessary for higher level competency.

ARITHMETIC

It is especially critical that from the earliest years basic arithmetic be taught in an incremental and cumulative manner and that students be allowed sufficient interaction with the material to achieve mastery. More than any other discipline, math is a cumulative exercise, building year by year. Students who have a "bad year" in math are likely to suffer for years as a result, and a mastery focus in the curriculum can help to ensure that students are not penalized because the school has low standards or inexact goals for student success. This means beginning with the simplest principles and sticking with them until they are thoroughly apprehended before moving to more complex principles.

As with reading, writing, and spelling skills, we are seeking *automaticity*. The basic skills should be second nature to our students so they are not hindered in tackling more complex computations by lack of facility in the basics. For younger students, and perhaps for older, the use of multiple modalities is imperative. Remember Hugo of St. Victor pacing off the geometric shapes on the floor of his room? This means that manipulatives and other tactile and kinesthetic tools should be an integral part of our pedagogy. Likewise, the rudiments of all the mathematical subdisciplines should be woven into the fabric of the early curriculum. Elementary principles of geometry, algebra, and statistics should be taught as soon as their foundational skills have been understood, along with understanding the calendar, timelines, and the analog clock.

Basic principles should be reinforced incrementally and cumulatively, so that things learned a week or a month ago are reviewed and tested again and again. This principle is antithetical to the organization of most published mathematics curricula that move from unit to unit as if every math principle is somehow isolated and independent of all others. If we allow our students to heave a sigh of relief because that terrible unit on fractions or negative numbers is behind us, we effectively doom them to struggle with mathematics throughout their educational careers.

There are not very many published examples of an incremental approach to teaching math, but one is worth mentioning. John Saxon realized that his students were frustrated with his algebra class because the text jumped from topic to topic without building upon previously mastered knowledge. He devised an incremental approach that had his students eagerly anticipating the quadratic equation because of their mastery of the elements of the formula in the preceding incremental lessons. Saxon believed students were not ready for complex principles until they had achieved automaticity with the simpler elements that naturally piece together to form the more complex principle or process. With this in mind, Saxon devised a curriculum that backs incremental learning down to fourth grade. His associates have since provided a program that backs his pedagogical approach down to kindergarten. In other words, he used a 12-K approach to curriculum development.

Incremental methods are sometimes maligned for three basic reasons. The repetitive pace tends to bore students whose brains have grown accustomed to the frenetic pace of images and sounds with which they are bombarded in contemporary technological culture. Students, parents, and even teachers can become frustrated with such methods because we too are accustomed to instant gratification in everything from fast-food delivery to instant access to the wealth of information available through the Internet. But important things cannot be condensed into thirty-second sound bites, and in the category of important things, mathematics tops the list. A second complaint is directly related to the first. Because the educational establishment has embraced a fast-paced, unit-to-unit approach, an incremental scope and sequence might lag behind the status quo on some standardized testing categories. Third, incremental programs like Saxon's can seem to work against a multi-modal approach to teaching and learning.

First, the question of a slower-paced instruction. The thorough apprehension of basic mathematics skills is so critical to overall academic success that we must take our thinking about its mastery to a higher level. The latest brain research is verifying what astute educators have known through experience and intuition for some time. The only way to move facts, concepts, and even physical dexterity from short-term to long-term memory (i.e., the only way to achieve automaticity) is by repetition. Modern brain researchers have actually observed that the brains of the best golfers, highly skilled musicians, and even professional chess players are significantly altered as compared to highly competent amateur practitioners of the same activities.[1] It would be ludicrous for the professional golfer, after making one beautiful lay-up to the pin, to say, "Okay, I have that skill down, now back to the long game." Similarly, the cellist who moved on to the next piece after one errorless rehearsal of her instrument's voice in one of Beethoven's string quartets is not necessarily destined for greatness. Research indicates that the difference between a competent amateur and a master performer is about twenty rehearsal hours per week. We all know that the way to Carnegie Hall is "practice, practice, practice," but a whole educational culture seems to have forgotten that the way to proficiency in any discipline is likewise, practice, practice, practice! Repetition is what it takes to develop our long-term memory, but most of us are too impatient to care.

As for standardized test results, it may be true that second-grade students in incremental math programs score below the national average on two out of twenty competency areas, but we have trouble being too concerned when the same students score in the 98th to 100th percentile on the other eighteen areas and when, by fourth grade, these same students "knock the socks off" students in faster-paced, unit-based programs. A school that really cares about and understands its curriculum should never be pressured to perform at certain levels on aspects of standardized tests that occur out of sequence with its own prescribed objectives.

The third issue that arises with programs that bite math processes off in small chunks is that some students need more frequent, concentrated, repetitive drill to ensure long-term memory. There is also the issue of finding space in the instructional sequence to spend time on applications of mathematical principles alongside abstract problem solving. Both of these problems can be addressed by a thorough knowledge of the curriculum objectives by every teacher and by the accompanying time and freedom to deviate from a published program to explore other avenues or modalities of comprehending and remembering what is being taught.

Which brings us back to the fact that a highly competent math faculty, who thoroughly comprehend the liberal arts approach to learning, may reject one curricular program (such as Saxon) in favor of another, but it should be on the basis of well-articulated objectives and a creatively devised instructional framework. At Regents School of Austin, the upper school math department has developed a set of standards and protocols for mastery that in their estimation transcend the various instructional programs, including Saxon and a host of more conventional series. Frustrated by years of watching students in conventional schools cram for tests, pad poor test grades with daily homework scores, and move from level to level without clearly demonstrating proficiency, the faculty devised a set of principles from which they derived a pedagogically sound approach to teaching and assessing their discipline.

Briefly, Regents's mastery program asserts that students should be able to demonstrate mastery in both computational skills and problem-solving applications if the curriculum goals, instruction, and assessment consistently reinforce both as essential, integrated elements of the program. A set of basic skills and applications has been devised for each level of math, and students must score consistently at a minimum level (substantially higher than passing) on basic skills and applications exams to matriculate to the next level or to receive credit. For some, this requires re-teaching, re-learning, and re-testing the skills and applications. But requiring mastery in both areas and strictly enforcing a standard of competence prevents the unhappy but all-too-common circumstance of students who have been promoted to higher levels of math but who lack the basic skills for success.

A further benefit to a robust mathematics program is that it increases the confidence of the science department in their efforts to engage students in lab-based, problem-solving-oriented science. Chemistry, physics, and microbiology become much less mysterious and frustrating to the ordinary student when the subject is not complicated by confusion over simple computational errors. The problem-solving aspect of the math mastery standard also lends itself to a higher level of integration between science and math, as the math department is always on the hunt for concrete problems from the sciences that students can solve with the math they are learning.

Another pressure that independent schools face with regard to mathematics instruction is also pace related but involves another aspect of brain research. Because students in early adolescence tend to develop at radically different rates (e.g., boys often lag behind girls for as many as eighteen months in both physical and cognitive development, and same-gender differences can be equally pronounced), a wide range of preparedness for abstract concepts can usually be detected within a class of students who are the same age. Students (especially boys) who are brilliant arithmeticians in fifth or sixth grade may flounder if they are pushed into algebra ahead of their cognitive ability to process the complexity of the discipline, especially as it is presented in most text series. This can be a frustration to parents who think that their "little genius" is losing ground academically by not being placed into the most advanced math at the earliest opportunity, but schools must exercise good judgment and not place students in situations that may ultimately frustrate them. In the long run, students appropriately placed will excel above those who aren't, and no college admissions counselor or employer ever asks, "How old were you when you first took algebra?" during the interview. This and the range of abilities exhibited by entering students almost certainly require testing and placing students in appropriate courses according to cognitive development and ability rather than according to age.

The good news is that with strategic upper school scheduling and proper curriculum development, students who begin algebra in ninth grade still have time for geometry, advanced algebra, trigonometry, and an introduction to calculus and statistics. This is preparation for college indeed, and following an incremental and cumulative approach (12-K) can, if necessary, meet the needs of every student in one track. However, it is also useful to recognize that there are thresholds of aptitude beyond eighth grade that good students may encounter, frustrating their further progress at other points in their careers. Just because a student traversed geometry and algebra II with dexterity does not mean that he or she will be able to make the leap to calculus while still in high school. Highly motivated, disciplined students may want to plunge into calculus for the sake of the college admissions transcript, but an observant math department or academic advisor may need to redirect a student's math interests toward additional studies in statistics or computer science to avoid a meltdown in the upper reaches of the math program. The school that provides upper-level math options other than calculus may do many ambitious students a valuable service, while still upholding a rigorous standard for all.

It should be noted, however, that calculus has tremendous value, not only for its power to develop conceptual thinking, but also as a practical tool for the natural and technical sciences. The student who intends to pursue physics, engineering, or even biomedical science will be helped along the way by a preparatory understanding of integral and differential mathematics. Nevertheless, the liberal arts approach, properly administered, will prepare our graduates to outpace their peers in college calculus and advanced mathematics well in time to succeed in any of the "math-heavy" sciences.

Still, it is worth noting that the more ubiquitous mathematical requirement for all people in all walks of life is statistics. An understanding of the basic principles of statistics will inform our students' ability to rightly judge the efficacy of the popular media's reporting of societal "trends" (what's that saying about liars and statisticians?) and will provide them with an important tool for wise decision-making. Statistical analysis forms the basis for data-based decision-making, a far more powerful approach to wise leadership and management than that typically employed in today's economic and political culture (i.e., experience and intuition alone). And yet statistics is the rarest mathematical discipline to be found in conventional schools. It is our opinion that the "complete" mathematical education will necessarily include at least some treatment of statistics.

Finally, given the growing role of computers in every dimension of modern life, our students need a basic understanding of the theory and operation of these machines. It is not sufficient for the young scholar to merely interact with a "black box" shrouded in mystery. Some understanding of computer logic, language, and operational systems will better prepare them to engage a culture that is increasingly at the mercy of its technology.

GEOMETRY

Because of its place in all our minds as a subdiscipline of mathematics, we have already addressed the inclusion of plane and solid geometry in the curriculum. But from ancient times geometry held its prominent place in the *quadrivium* because of its broad implications concerning all spatial interrelations. Geometry forms the basis for our understanding of how we relate to and interact with the physical world and has endless implications for our apprehension of truth, goodness, and beauty.

We have included geography under this mathematical art, as did the ancients. The importance of geography to the curriculum from the earliest years is tremendous. Not only does a student's growing understanding of geography assist him in "finding" himself in his neighborhood, community, region, nation, and world, but such understanding also is essential to his apprehension of God's providence in human history and culture, both of which have been shaped (if not dictated) by the great geological formations throughout the world. No history lesson or study of any great work of literature is complete without locating for our students and teaching them the habit of locating the places of relevance on the map. As we have indicated before, an early, thorough, and continuing understanding of geography is essential to a quality education.

Finally, we include under geometry the visual arts. It is likely that the fine arts in general are the most neglected of the disciplines in the conventional school curriculum. Many schools, public and private, tend to treat the fine arts as extracurricular or (even worse!) as "specials." The implication is that these exist outside of the normal core of the formal curriculum. On the contrary, it is particularly fitting that the Christian school expose students both to the study and creation of art. Our students must learn how they can adapt and how others have adapted God's creative nature expressed through his image-bearers. Furthermore, engagement in the fine arts is essential to brain development, and students who employ the visual arts for their own sake as well as for learning other disciplines will find greater ease in learning. For example, it has long been an essential exercise in the science of natural history to sketch what one observes in the laboratory or in nature. Likewise, it is impossible to gain an appropriate understanding of history and culture without attending to the expressions of these, preserved for us in the form of art.

The rudiments of architecture, likewise, should not be neglected. Architecture is powerfully reflective of the sense of truth, goodness, and beauty held by cultures otherwise forgotten. Students must come to see how form follows function and feel for themselves how, for example, the use of certain materials and of sheer space in great libraries and cathedrals draws the mind and heart toward learning and worship.

We firmly maintain that the fine arts are fundamental to the liberal arts approach to educating students, and that schools must prioritize their resources so that the students' experience is permeated with artistic activities. The range of programming options is nearly infinite, so we will not try to prescribe a scope and sequence here. But we do suggest that curriculum planning in the fine arts be subjected to the same 12-K process as for all other subjects. What will be the impact of your school's fine arts program on the students who become your alumni? To what extent will you provide for their development as practitioners and patrons of the arts? Will the school educate painters, sculptors, photographers, and videographers as part of its artistic mission? To what extent will the arts be integrated into the curriculum goals of other disciplines like the humanities and the sciences, and to what extent will students be required to reference the arts to perform successfully in those disciplines?

As a school answers these questions and others like them, a vision of its artistic end products will emerge. Each activity from 12 to K ought to be focused on achieving these goals, thus making each artistic activity essential to the scope and sequence of the curriculum.

THE NATURAL SCIENCES

The sciences may be the pivotal area of study that has, for decades, thrust thinking Christian parents into a dilemma as to whether their children are best served by receiving a Christian education or by gaining the benefits of a quality education, as if the two were mutually exclusive. The sad reality is that for a very long time in most communities the local Christian school provided what many considered a physically, emotionally, and spiritually safe environment while caring little for the rigors of a challenging academic experience.

Meanwhile, for many evangelicals, the science versus religion debate has raged on as if these too were mutually exclusive. As to the latter, the simple solution is the logical one: when science and religion appear to conflict, there is a problem with our interpretation of one or the other or perhaps with both. This has proven the case since Galileo's day and is still the case when it comes to educating students in the liberal arts tradition. Our students must learn the foundational skills necessary for both sound biblical and data interpretation. As to the former, the dichotomy between quality and Christian education has been a driving force in the recovery of the Christian liberal arts as an approach to learning that, necessarily, is both.

The overarching paradigm for a Christian education in the sciences is the understanding that our worldview embraces the reality that our study of the natural sciences is our window into God's revelation of himself to his image-bearers through his creation. To paraphrase Francis Bacon, "God has given us two books by which to know him; the book of his Word [the Scriptures] and the book of his World [Creation] and it is incumbent upon us to study both!" Another Francis—Schaeffer—was one of the first modern evangelicals to point to the historical reality that the Western tradition of science derived from the Christian worldview that dominated Europe between 400 and 1600 A.D. Though many of the early modern scientists like da Vinci and Bacon asserted a high degree of independence from the Christian thinking of their day, the framework within which they sought to investigate, know, and describe the world around them was unequivocally Christian.

The key to approaching topics that are controversial (in science or any other discipline) is, to borrow an analogy from science, inoculation, not quarantine. We do not want to insulate our students from the ideas that pervade the university and the broader culture, but rather expose them to these ideas and let them exercise their dialectic skills upon them while they are still under our tutelage. If we have done our job properly, our graduates will have the wisdom to distinguish truth from error and will have the eloquence to articulate the distinction to their professors, fellow students, and the general public as the opportunities present themselves.

As we have said of other disciplines, the sciences should be taught "as science," and students must learn to think like scientists when doing their science. This means that observation, experimentation and data gathering, interpretation, and presentation must be part of the educational experience from the very earliest instruction to the conclusion of our 12-K program. For many of our schools, the clustering of grades 10-12 may be appropriate for instruction in the sciences so that students may take biology, chemistry, and physics in any order and so that tenth and twelfth graders may take the same class together. There is certainly a scheduling benefit to such an approach, but the science faculty may have valid academic objections. For example, it will be important for students to have a sufficiently strong background in mathematics in order to fare well in physics. However, a curious quirk in conventional education regarding the sciences is the traditional sequencing of biology, chemistry, and physics in alphabetical order. The reality, as every college science professor knows, is that students require a basic understanding of chemistry in order to properly apprehend biology, and similarly students require a certain understanding of physics to properly apprehend chemistry. The obvious arrangement of these disciplines (given a sufficient background in mathematics) becomes physics, then chemistry, then biology, but schools must weigh all the variables in establishing their own science curriculum and schedule.

MUSIC

Again, we acknowledge the surprise some may experience by the inclusion of music in the mathematical arts. Yet music is thoroughly arithmetical, from its tones and octaves to its use of rhythm and time to its harmonic frequencies. Further, it is well understood that facility in either math or music facilitates ease of learning in the other. Such facility for the two is best gained simultaneously.

Further still, modern brain research has determined that activities requiring concentration, like studying or performing surgery, are enhanced when the practitioner is listening to certain music (think Vivaldi's *Four Seasons*, not Puff Daddy's *Think I'm Jiggy*).[2] The importance of music to the curriculum cannot be exaggerated, and, again, the earlier music education begins, the better prepared the student will be for a wide range of learning. Like all the fine arts, the 12-K approach must dictate the progression of musical instruction, but the complete program will weave elements of music history, appreciation, theory, and performance into every level of instruction. And music should be required for every student every year. The richest school music program (there may be a double entendre here) will offer concert band (orchestra and/or ensemble), chorus, and individual performance opportunities for its students, beginning in fourth grade and continuing to graduation, with instruction in the lower grades that is preparatory to such programming. The challenge for the smaller school is that such diverse offerings may require two or more teachers, having differing expertise. In any case, music is essential to our kind of learning, and within reason, the more the better!

Included in music are dance and sport (*gymnasia*). In fact, certain forms of dance may be viewed as sport and credited accordingly. Despite the obvious controversy that dance may cause for some schools, it can be a real joy to see young men and women expressing God's truth, goodness, and beauty through dance, either separately or together, having learned deep respect both for the art and for each other. Schools that sponsor proms or cotillions may do well to offer formal instruction each year in real dance steps and in the art of standard dance in its various forms prior to this important event.

As to sport (or athletics, so called), it has long been the tradition at most independent college preparatory schools to require every student to participate in one interscholastic sport each season. We are inclined to support this notion of student responsibility in keeping with the liberal arts tradition. From the time of Plato, sport (or *gymnasia*) has been central to the curriculum and not relegated to the status of extracurricular. If this is to be the condition of sport at our schools, we must again take the 12-K approach to educating our students in this art.

Since facility in two or three sports is likely our goal for our graduates, we must begin instruction in sport from the earliest years. This precludes a "President's Council for Physical Fitness" approach to P.E. Instead, students should learn the rules of the various games and rehearse the basic physical skills that are necessary to execute when playing the games effectively. Dexterity with ball, racket, mallet, bat, club, stick, foil, gloves, oar, and puck and on the field, court, ring, water, ice, fairway, green, and saddle will be the focus.

THE TRUE SCIENCES

If we understand the word *science* to mean "knowledge" in its ancient and medieval contexts, then theology and philosophy represent the true knowledge toward which all our studies in the liberal arts has been building. The facility we have gained with language through grammar, dialectic, and rhetoric and that we have gained with the *mathemata* through arithmetic, geometry, natural science, and music, herein described, and the linguistic skills, research skills, analytical skills, thinking skills, and communication skills all work together to aid us in our understanding of God, his world, ourselves, and our fellows. The skills, knowledge, and virtues we have gained empower us to leverage this understanding in making meaningful contributions to society and in being "culture makers," who purposefully shape their contemporary culture rather than passively experience or, worse still, simply observe it.

Theology and philosophy, from ancient times, were the disciplines that "got at" the cosmic issues of origin and meaning. The liberal arts education we have labored to impart to our students is not complete without at least a survey of these. By now, you are tired of reading these words, but as with all learning in our approach, we must back it down 12-K. Even though the "true sciences" represent the pinnacle of preparatory learning (remember, their study preceded the professional disciplines like medicine and law), like all the disciplines, their rudiments must be tackled early and be built upon throughout the curriculum.

Of course, every Christian school curriculum includes a study of the Bible, but here we must be careful. Some have argued that because of the diversity of denominations represented in most Christian schools, responsibility for Bible instruction should be left to parents and the church. This is an extreme application of our principle that schools are schools (cf. chapter 3), and we cannot support it. However, it does raise the legitimate question of "what approach to Bible learning is most appropriate to the liberal arts curriculum?"

Many schools have adopted the goal of having the Scriptures at the "center of all instruction," but this could mean many things. For our purposes, we will use the Scriptures as the measure by which all other learning is weighed. For our older scholars this will mean judging all human ideas and actions in light of biblical principles. Whether these ideas and actions are encountered in our study of history, philosophy, science, or psychology (to name a few), their ultimate value will hinge upon our viewing them, as Calvin said, through the "spectacles of the Scriptures." This requires that teachers effectively integrate their knowledge of the Bible and Christian doctrine with the various disciplines they teach, and it requires that students themselves are gaining an increasing familiarity with the Bible's contents and themes.

Two tendencies in teaching the Bible need to be balanced in the Christian liberal arts school so that teachers don't fall into the ditch on either side of the narrow road of integrating the Scriptures with other disciplines. The first "ditch" is a preoccupation with "application." The goal of an "application"-oriented approach to teaching the Bible is to consistently confront students with the demands of the gospel upon their lives. To avoid hard-heartedness or the risk of cold, dead knowledge, we constantly remind students that we have to respond to what the Scriptures teach with repentance and obedience. If we are not careful, this approach can become trite and, if it is at all contrived, may inoculate our students to the gospel rather than warming them to it. Employed exclusively, this approach tends to avoid teaching the parts of the Bible from which moral lessons cannot easily be distilled, robbing our students of some of the more important theological content in the Bible.

The second "ditch" is a preoccupation with "academics." An exclusively "academic" approach avoids application altogether, contenting us with the transference of information. There is nothing inherently wrong with teaching the Bible as an academic subject, but we do run the risk of our biblical instruction becoming just one more course for students to endure. Ideally, we must strike a balance between the two approaches. Such a balance is problematic for many schools, which relegate Bible instruction to teacher discretion, leading to a haphazard treatment of the Scriptures that may jump back and forth between whole years of application and academics as students move from teacher to teacher.

The easiest way to avoid leaning too heavily one way or the other is (say it with us) to teach the Bible 12-K and in different contexts with different goals in mind. It is appropriate for the seventh-grade Bible course, for example, to include heavy doses of archaeology and Semitic cultural studies if that is not the students' only exposure to the Scriptures. Surprising students with serious, uncontrived references to Scripture in courses like math or spelling also helps to cement the impression that the Bible is wholly relevant to the entire range of academic pursuits.

In the end, we hope to have trained our students to orient their conclusions about the world and its ways around the Scriptures. As students mature, biblical study can expand to broader philosophical considerations. A planned curriculum that demonstrates how biblical thinking should be applied to cultural concerns is vital, and, as with any other discipline, the more "real-world" the context, the greater the impact.

In this regard, we do not necessarily contend that teaching the Bible or theology in a set of courses separate from other disciplines is necessarily the best way for theology and biblical content to enter the students' experience. Separate coursework can certainly be more efficient, but if any of the other faculty or departments are tempted to abdicate their responsibility to shape students' worldviews through their own discipline, then tragic damage has been done to the entire prospect of Christian education in the liberal arts tradition. In either case, a robust theological curriculum will include Old and New Testament surveys, hermeneutics, ethics, church history, comparative religions, and both systematic and biblical theology. How to organize all this into the whole-school curriculum will be the challenge that each school must address.

For younger students, Bible memory and recitation will be an important exercise, along with rehearsing the books and important people of the Bible. And integrating biblical history and geography into the curriculum for these disciplines will increase the relevance of Bible stories to the broader scope of world studies and vice versa. For memory learning to have greatest relevance for future learning, whole passages should be learned in context, building for our youngest learners a verse at a time until all of Psalm 23, Psalm 100, Deuteronomy 20, and James 5, for example, can be quoted from memory.

But Bible alone is not a sufficient beginning to our students' learning in theology. In keeping with the liberal arts tradition, we recommend that our developing theologians be "treated" to catechesis: the corporate antiphonal rehearsal of questions and answers about basic Christian doctrine. The Old-World catechisms from Italy, Byzantium, England, Scotland, and Germany have proven their value for systematic instruction in doctrine for centuries. In our experience, they have been deeply appreciated by parents of all denominations, despite their historic usage in just a few. Additionally, we believe the ancient creeds of the Christian church to be invaluable for our students, since they provide them with succinct summaries of the foundational beliefs of the Christian faith.

The study of philosophy and, in our modern context, psychology and sociology can wait until the later years of the curriculum, but exposure to the people and both the great and heretical ideas that have emerged through these disciplines will be critical to our students' preparation for college and our culture. Understanding how such ideas have influenced everything from political change (e.g., American, French, and Bolshevik Revolutions) to medical care to marketing toothpaste and subjecting them, in turn, to the scrutiny of biblical principles may be among the most important college preparatory lessons our students will learn.

eight

THE RHETORIC CURRICULUM

WE HAVE ADDRESSED the issue of curriculum development in a very general sense in the foregoing chapters. Believing a fuller discipline-by-discipline curriculum development to be beyond the scope of this volume, we offer in this chapter an example of the recommended thorough development of the curriculum for just one of the liberal arts disciplines. We have identified rhetoric for this example for two important reasons. First, we believe rhetoric to be the overarching discipline for the purposeful formation of wise and eloquent servants in a postmodern age. Second, it occurs to us that the area for which most schools may require special guidance in curriculum development is that of integrating principles of rhetoric into the elementary program. Without the help of the rare teacher who has been exposed to a historical treatment of this discipline as part of an advanced degree program, it is unlikely that the typical school would stumble upon these principles. Yet, there is perhaps no more important challenge before our schools' faculty in shaping students who will be both wise and eloquent.

THE CASE FOR RHETORIC

During the period following the formal proposal of the *trivium* as three separate disciplines through which students progress, much of European thinking was dominated by scholastic philosophers and theologians. The rise of scholasticism (illustrated by the writings of Anselm, Duns Scotus, Aquinas, and others) was accompanied by the reintroduction of Aristotelian principles to Western thinking. The result was a highly formalized, technical pursuit of understanding through natural, rational means. Logical constructions were understood to be authoritative and bound the thinking of most Christians—even, occasionally, in opposition to the authority of the Scriptures. In this context, dialectical thinking and formal logic naturally held center stage as the most important medium for teaching and learning.

Whereas rhetorical skill had been the mark of the truly educated and gifted leader during the classical period and late antiquity, the high medieval period reduced the role of the rhetorician to official correspondent. Logicians, not rhetoricians, were called on to defend the interests of church and state, and those trained in rhetoric were mainly responsible to add style to official pronouncements made by bishops and the landed gentry. The place of rhetoric in the medieval academy was secondary at best, optional at worst. Classical rhetoric was and is particularly suited to persuade people who are presented with at least two mutually exclusive courses of action. In the highly centralized and largely monarchic environment of medieval Europe, the need to persuade large numbers of influential people was rare, and Sayers's explication of the *trivium* reflected this historical bias.

The Renaissance marked a shift in academic approach from deductive, authoritative arguments within strictly defined parameters to the comparative study of texts and traditions as the new wave of humanism swelled. In this context, rhetoricians were once again needed to sort out the various competing religious and political options. For the first time in centuries, atheism was becoming a fairly commonly held conviction among educated people, and the absolute rule or "divine right" of kings was being challenged by the prosperity and influence of a very large population of merchants and political activists.

Fast-forward seven hundred years. The twentieth century saw one traditional Western institution after another deconstructed by a new line of reasoning that attacked traditional authority and cultural conventions, turning much of society on its ear. It was a dialectical war that most traditionalists in religion and government were largely unprepared for and that they consequently lost.

So at the beginning of the twenty-first century we have found that traditional forms of public discourse were overturned decades before. Logical argumentation has little effect on those who do not accept the conventional rules of absolute truth, and very few in our society, even among the educated, have the mental discipline to engage in detailed philosophical conversations, the conclusions of which depend on basic cause-and-effect assumptions. Enter rhetoric once again.

While rhetoric makes use of logic, its effectiveness does not depend on an audience's acceptance of airtight, deductive arguments. The skilled rhetorician is not intimidated by the sloppy thinking of her or his audience but relishes the opportunity to shape their thinking and behavior using a variety of means. Where the logician is stymied by an audience who responds to sound arguments with a resounding, "That might be true for you . . ." the rhetorician is equipped to take up the challenge of persuasion and to continue a profitable discourse, even when facing the most stubborn anti-rationalist.

Rhetoric also provides the greatest opportunity for educating morally aware students and for using the classroom to propagate character. We established in an earlier chapter that liberal arts schooling always seeks to educate the conscience and that liberal arts thinking blended with Christian theology promises the greatest opportunity for genuine character education. Of the three elements of the *trivium*, rhetoric is most helpful in the construction of a total curriculum with character formation and cultural leadership as its chief goals.

THE RHETORICAL SCHOOL—INVERTING THE *TRIVIUM*

The great challenge facing the teacher who seeks to employ rhetoric as the guide to a total curriculum paradigm is to identify a set of rhetorical practices that allow students to develop a meaningful facility with words and arguments. Further, these training tools need to closely approximate the sorts of persuasive discourse common to contemporary culture. The principles of classical rhetoric are universal, but to strictly imitate training regimens designed by Greek and Roman orators seems arcane. Bland imitation of archaic forms may ultimately provoke distaste in students for a discipline critical to their success in the modern world.

Formal rhetorical instruction in the Hellenized world was accomplished in the context of learning all the things that cultural leaders of the day were required to know. All the liberal arts (and to some extent, the true sciences) were coordinated by the goal of producing orators who understood themselves, their fellow citizens, the historical values of their society, and what would be required to pursue the greater good in the future. Cicero argued that the practice of rhetoric executed a wide demand upon its students. Effective rhetoric urges a comprehensive knowledge of a variety of subjects; "a knowledge of very many matters must be grasped, without which oratory is but an empty and ridiculous swirl of verbiage." He continues to describe the need for vocabulary, a sense of style, an understanding of psychology, humor, wit, "culture befitting a gentleman," a warlike mind-set, "the whole being combined with a delicate charm and urbanity,"[1] all of which points up the need for an education in the liberal arts. In the modern school, a limited understanding of rhetoric as a discipline hampers this challenge, but the shortsighted objectives of most conventional schools also further complicate the challenge. If our job as teachers is merely to prepare students for college or the job market, we can hardly expect our teaching style to require them to become eloquent and wise.

A further challenge is to ensure that rhetorical instruction keeps as its center the goal of producing the noble citizen. As we have already seen, the Christian rhetorical context defines the ideal citizen as one who is capable of commerce not only in the "here-and-now" (that is, in the midst of Augustine's City of Man), but also one who understands himself or herself to inhabit the City of God. So, the "perfect orator" will be a good man or woman motivated by the pursuit of the transcendent principles of truth and justice in the world.

There has always been considerable debate over the value of technical exercises to the teaching of rhetoric. Some maintain, with good reason, that attention to technical details inevitably succumbs to the tendency to reduce rhetoric to stylistic mechanics. Augustine himself cautioned older students not to allow formal rhetorical education to interfere with their study of the Scriptures. He believed that rhetorical skill could be acquired through the careful observation and imitation of eloquent speakers without a formal understanding of academic principles of oratory. At the same time, however, the appropriate uses of language and argument are learned behaviors and must be modeled upon some example of effectiveness. While the mundane and archaic should be avoided, it is always helpful for the student of anything to begin with a model worth imitating. So, by providing our students with formal instruction in rhetoric and introducing rhetoric into their academic careers at an early point, we guarantee greater familiarity with rhetorical principles that, in turn, will fashion more eloquent students.

Teachers need to be trained to be alert to examples of effective modern oratory or persuasive writing, and to combine these models with their formal forays into rhetorical principles. Students need to be able to appreciate effective rhetoric and to analyze it academically. Their own imitation of effective persuasive discourse should be based on the recognition of principles, not just an instinctive aping of appealing styles.

In illustration of this point, in 1998 I (Littlejohn) gave the convocation address at a Christian liberal arts college, welcoming new and returning students to the campus community and challenging students and faculty alike toward a fresh commitment to pursue the renewing of their minds through the study of God's general and special revelations. My family joined me for the event, and at dinner that night, not convinced that he had listened, I invited my son (a rising high school junior with two years of classical rhetoric under his belt) to critique my message. To my surprise and great pleasure, he provided a most salient summary of the content, followed by an analysis of the rhetorical structure, and concluded with some pointers on how I could have better made my points through the inclusion of a few strategically placed rhetorical devices. As did Augustine's older students, I learned my rhetoric by observation and imitation. I have since heard my son address large audiences on several occasions, and I am convinced that his formal training in rhetoric has made him a more eloquent speaker than his father. But had he begun his rhetorical instruction earlier in his school experience, as we here advocate, his ease in acquiring rhetorical skills would doubtless have been even greater.

RHETORIC IN THE GRAMMAR SCHOOL

The tradition of *progymnasmata* (pronounced *pro-gim-náhz-ma-ta*), or the preliminary exercises for the practice of rhetoric, has both guided the historic development of rhetorical pedagogy and informs our understanding of its place in the modern curriculum. On the one hand, it is helpful to see how elementary rhetorical principles were introduced, for example, by the Byzantine rhetoricians to students of the discipline. This hopefully assists us as we try to envision the role that rhetoric and rhetoricians played in the development of the culture. The history of *progymnasmata* also instructs us as we seek to appreciate the various emphases that developed at different periods within rhetoric itself to address the linguistic needs of politicians, churchmen, and intellectuals.

On the other hand, regarding the place of rhetoric in the modern curriculum, we look for rhetoric's universal applicability in the forms of the *progymnasmata*. What is the current usefulness of training students in these ancient forms of composition and speech? A careful study of these exercises uncovers an approach to teaching persuasive composition and speech that actually feels very contemporary. Most teachers who have taught elementary or middle school composition will recognize some of the basic forms that are still taught in education classes. Additionally, several of the forms are designed to instruct students in moral reasoning—character education. So, the question that faces us as we rediscover the *progymnasmata* is direct: How can a modern school, taking on the task to shape wise and eloquent citizens, use these instructional forms to aid our students?

The earliest of the ancient *progymnasmata* were developed by Theon in the first century A.D. and Hermogenes in the second century. These were ultimately superseded in popular use by Aphthonius' contribution to the genre in the fourth century. Little is known about Aphthonius, but translations of his original Greek work into Latin were being made as late as 1665. Aphthonius represents a continuous attempt to make the basic forms of rhetoric accessible to teachers of young students who, for the most part, have not yet begun their formal training as rhetoricians. Before any student was handed Aristotle or Cicero, he spent years cutting his rhetorical teeth on the *progymnasmata*.

The goal of the forms was not to produce robotic speechmakers but rather to provide a comfortable structure within which an expressive student could "develop his own individuality."[2] The goal of the *progymnasmata* is confident composition. To that end, the prescribed forms must be firm, though not absolute.

The *progymnasmata* also support the premise earlier presented that the *trivium* is, and always has been, properly considered an overlapping instrument of instruction. These rhetorical preliminary exercises are designed for use with children as young as five or six. Before a student can read, he can memorize and can therefore be introduced to the *pro-*

gymnasmata, effectively making him a student of rhetoric. All grammatical and dialectical study, then, can be understood as both preliminary to and concurrent with the student's preparation as an orator who knows the good when he sees it, who is willing to do it, and who is capable of drawing others after him in pursuit of it.

AN AUGUSTINIAN PARADIGM FOR ELOQUENCE

So, let's propose some criteria for our contemporary *progymnasmata*. A rhetorical curriculum should facilitate the following skills:

1. Discernment and composition of useful arguments (Aristotle's "seeing the means of persuasion").
2. The use of contestable theses in discourse (the "need for persuasion").
3. An expansive understanding of discourse's applicability ("in any situation, whatever").
4. Familiarity with accepted patterns of discourse (e.g., deliberative, forensic, and epideictic compositions; topics; invention and arrangement of arguments).
5. Facility in basic mechanics of composition and speech (style, memory, presentation).

Having established that rhetoric was understood by its most prominent proponents to be a suitable context for the training of character, we look to Augustine for the sense of what should constitute this character-focused rhetorical program. We can surmise these four things:

1. The primary obligation of oratory is to truth, understood as a combination of authoritative revelation and reasoned reflection upon that revelation.
2. Classical principles of rhetoric are dependable and useful.
3. Successful oratory is largely evaluated by its persuasive effect.
4. The most persuasive element of rhetoric is the orator's good life.

Each exercise that we propose, then, should incorporate as many of these elements as possible, the goal being that students should gain the benefit of both wisdom and eloquence.

WISDOM *and* ELOQUENCE

AN UPDATED APHTHONIUS

Elementary Exercises

1. MYTHOS

Mythos (or "fable") is a mythological story communicating some moral lesson. The possible forms are "verbal" or "ethical." The former consists of a story in which the moral is spoken. The latter is a story in which the moral is demonstrated or found in the action of the myth. The rhetorical purpose of fables is twofold: first, to pass along some important moral truth to the young student, and second, to begin training the memory and oratorical presence. The student memorizes a well-written myth, word for word, and presents it for the edification of an audience.

For young students, memorizing and reciting moral lessons provides a compelling opportunity to learn 1) conventional styles of composition that will be internalized and imitated unconsciously, 2) illustrated moral and theological truth, and 3) two of the five crucial elements of classical rhetoric: memory and presentation.[3] *Mythos* exercises also take advantage of and strengthen the elementary-age student's facility for memorization. But the exercise provides the student the opportunity to memorize for the purpose of instructing others, rather than just memorizing material for his own benefit.

Here are some examples of fables for memory and recitation:

a. Well-told, short Bible stories. (Jesus' parable of the Good Samaritan is a good example of a moral lesson that is structured so it is easy to remember—straightforward plot, repetitive action, only a few characters, and very little dialogue.)

b. Aphthonius assumes the use of Aesop's fables. From an Augustinian perspective, Aesop might need editing to communicate a consistently Christian moral, but it can be done with little effort.

c. Short stories of famous inventions. (Benjamin Franklin's discovery of electricity, Archimedes' discovery of displacement—Eureka!—to demonstrate the orderliness of creation and the potential for human ingenuity.)

d. Civic myths. (George Washington and the cherry tree, Paul Revere's ride, Nathan Hale's self-sacrifice in war, Florence Nightingale's example of personal risk for the sake of compassion.)

Since fables will be a mixture of true stories and fiction, we prefer the Greek term *mythos* to help young minds distinguish between the genre, on the one hand, and the truth or fiction of the story on the other. Fable implies fiction, but the Greek *mythos* has a much broader connotation, including both true and fictitious events that are critical to our Western cultural identity.

Mythos should, of course, be shorter for very young children and should gradually lengthen with their increasing age and ability to keep memorized information straight. Narrative poems might also be used, and short *mythos* can be easily composed by creative teachers, or by older students with editing help from teachers.

2. TALE

The Greek world for *tale* is, literally, a leading through. This is a combined composition/recitation exercise designed to help the student see the essential elements of a plot and to summarize them in an interesting way. Aphthonius' goals for the student-composed tale are: clarity, brevity, believability, and conventional styling.

Three types of tale are to be used: dramatic, historical, and political. The dramatic takes a short piece of imaginative literature (Aphthonius suggests "the forging of Achilles' armor" from Homer's *Iliad*) and abstracts it according to the above criteria. Historical topics are those traditional stories told by the ancients. Political tales should be those things, Aphthonius says, actually practiced by legal orators practicing for their cases. Examples of tales to be retold might be:

a. Dramatic—Aeneas' flight from Troy, the death of Hamlet, popular short stories, etc. The goal should be to expose students to relatively short bursts of mature storytelling and to require them to tell just as pleasing a tale in their own words, given the four criteria.

b. Historical—David and Goliath, Elijah's contest with the prophets of Baal, any of the lengthier accounts of Jesus' miracles, the fall of Rome, the heroics of St. Patrick, the death of Roland, etc. The goal should be to help students see both the story and its importance to our understanding of the characters and us.

c. Political—This topic proves more difficult. We have little access to the actual transcripts of classical orators, and what we have, say of the speeches of Isocrates or Gorgias, is largely ornamental and not really legal in nature. A recounting of Socrates' defense or of Jesus' various trials might get at the intention somewhat. Seneca, of course, provides sample scenarios for rhetoric students to practice on, some of them quite outrageous. Another option would be to get the transcript of a well-conducted modern trial (e.g., Scopes or Vanzetti) and have students digest and abstract the major arguments in story fashion. While requiring more creativity on the teacher's part, the exercise could be very fruitful, especially for advanced or older students.

In addition to the skills acquired through this exercise, students are offered digestible pieces of mature literature, which familiarizes them with classic stories and authors. Tale also provides the opportunity to interpret this literature through the lens of moral and theological discernment at an early age:

> When Aeneas flees Troy with his crippled father and the family idols on his back, what does this tell us about what was important to Aeneas? Yes, he demonstrated courage and love for his father, and that is to be commended and imitated. But we also understand that Aeneas' capacity for love was incomplete, since the gods he trusted were false, and he had no divine example of pure love to follow.

3. PROVERBS AND MAXIMS

Aphthonius next prescribes the examination and exegesis of proverbs and maxims. The English understanding of these two forms of wisdom is more useful than the Greek. While both are short, pithy statements, a proverb is ordinarily understood to be stating something ordinary to practical human experience (e.g., "A word to the wise is sufficient"), while a maxim is more commonly a brief, memorable statement of a principle of conduct or morality (e.g., "When in doubt, don't"). Aphthonius further distinguishes between the two by requiring that a proverb be attributable to a known source (Solomon, Socrates, etc.).

More important than the forms themselves, however, is Aphthonius' prescription for their use. His goal is to give the student practice in analyzing and critiquing something of obvious cultural value—to think in an original way about something famously assumed already to be true. Eight modes in which to understand and explain a proverb or maxim are suggested. Each mode can be prescribed as individual (brief) paragraphs or in combination as a longer speech. (Again, I do not think it is unreasonable to expect younger students to learn the Greek-based titles of these modes, as any English rendering will be cumbersome and may contribute more to confusion than clarity.) These are the modes:

a. Encomiastic—a paragraph praising the merits and credibility of the author (in the case when the author is known).

b. Paraphrastic—explaining the meaning of the proverb or maxim in the student's own words.

c. Causative—explaining more fully the forces that ensure that this proverb or maxim will indeed be borne out.

d. Reversative—explaining what will happen if the proverb or maxim is not heeded, or describing circumstances contrary to those described in the statement.

e. Parabolic—inventing an analogy that helps to illustrate the truth stated.

f. Paradigmatic—an example of a person or circumstance that has shown the truth of the claim.

g. Witness of the ancients—reminding the audience of dependable sources who have also claimed this statement to be true.

h. Epilogue—a final entreaty not to ignore the truth contained in the proverb or maxim.

Proverbs and maxims provide an excellent means of engraining basic cultural assumptions into the consciousness of impressionable students. Whether a school's intention is to train students in generic principles like the Protestant work ethic ("Early to bed, early to rise makes a man healthy, wealthy and wise"—Benjamin Franklin, proverb) or to teach theological and moral principles ("Do unto others as you would have them do unto you"—Jesus, maxim), the power of these short, memorable truth statements is undeniable.

From a pedagogical point of view, the ability to explain the meaning and relevance of a commonly understood cultural tenet is invaluable to the orator's dialectical responsibility to see the point of an argument—a critical rhetorical skill of *invention*. These simple exercises also follow easily on the skills of abstraction gained in previous exercises retelling famous stories, with the added dimension of analysis to provoke higher-order thinking. Further, proverbs and maxims are universal forms that provide tremendous opportunities for the comparison of values between cultures.

Consider the following:

• Confucius said, "A noble man is not a utensil."

• Paul said, "If anyone cleanses himself from what is dishonorable, he will be a vessel for honorable use."

The analysis of these proverbs will not only encourage students to appreciate different shades of meaning in the same words, but it also opens up an opportunity to compare and contrast the understandings of self inherent in both Chinese and Christian European cultures. Students benefit from exercises in analysis, composition, and presentation; the teacher benefits from a segue provided to introduce two very different but critically important cultural understandings in the modern world.

In relation to rhetoric as a discipline, proverbs and maxims provide a useful introduction to the formal use of topics in the process of invention (the formal preparation of arguments for use in composition). The task of the rhetorician is to see the available means of persuasion, and the classical topics have been one of the most popular means of generating the ideas that great orators need to compose their compelling arguments.[4]

4. CONFIRMATION AND REFUTATION[5]

If the heart of rhetoric is persuasion, then nothing is more important than developing the arguments that will move an audience to become receptive to the reasonableness and the probable truth of the orator's point. Learning to confirm and refute arguments is indispensable to the rhetorician's competence. While many students are born with a talent for stylistic eloquence (the "gift of gab"), very few are inherently logical and careful thinkers. Exercises in the confirmation and refutation of arguments help train students' thinking toward independent discernment.

Successful confirmation and refutation at an elementary level depends on the student's methodical use of topics (introduced above). While this might seem wooden and uncreative, the student must be trained in an orderly method of thinking.[6] The topics prescribed by Aphthonius help ensure that the student's foundation in invention is firm. Confirmation and refutation also correspond to Ciceronian principles defining the essential elements of a discourse. So these exercises really mark the students' entrance into the formal study of rhetoric and are something of a rite of passage.

The language Aphthonius employs has to do with building and dismantling. His emphasis is on the strength of one's analysis and argument. Each of these exercises, he says, "encompasses within itself all the power of the art." It is the rhetorician's duty to construct an indestructible argument, meanwhile looking for the weakness that will bring his opponent's assertions toppling down. As a rule, the orator avoids proving or disproving anything that is obvious ("overly plain") or absurd ("completely impossible"). Rather, the clever orator must concentrate on the middle ground, especially the area in which an audience might easily be confused or be found to assume the truth of a commonly held falsehood.

Narration is mainly the process of defining the relevant issues and terms of an argument so as to gain an advantage with the audience. The orator praises the ethical qualities and reasonableness of those who agree with him and disparages the abilities of those who disagree.

The topics are prescribed in parallel fashion:

Confirmation	Refutation
1. Praise the good reputation of the proponent.	1. State the false assertion of the opponent.
2. Explain/narrate the matter.	2. Explain/narrate the matter.
3. Point out the obvious merits of the argument.	3. Show the obscurity of the opposition.
4. Demonstrate how many have been convinced.	4. Accentuate the incredible properties.
5. Prove that the position is entirely probable:	5. Show the impossibility of the position:
a. It is consistent.	a. It is inconsistent.
b. It is proper or appropriate.	b. It is unbecoming.
c. It is reasonable.	c. It is irrational.

To practice, Aphthonius recommends that the student analyze a commonly known myth and argue for or against its probability. The exercise as he describes it becomes somewhat cumbersome and approaches the absurd, but the effect is that the student must struggle with the topics in order to make a sound argument.[7] Another option is

to have students analyze a debate in parts, forming their own confir-
mations and refutations and comparing them to the original (as in the
Athenian debate between Cleon and Diodotus over the fate of the rebel-
lious Mitylenians). To begin, students should be given something of
either obvious truth or falsehood so that they can practice using the topics to argue a point nearly conceded. As the skill of the students
increases, so should the ambiguity of the judgments and arguments they
are asked to make.

In using these topics to construct or demolish arguments, students
will find it useful to have already learned some elementary dialectical
skills. For instance, students should know how to discern between an
issue that should not be argued (e.g., a matter of public record) and a
matter open for discussion. It also will help students to have learned the
basic rules of deductive arguments and to be able to critique and construct simple syllogisms.

5. PRAISE AND CENSURE[8]

Praise and censure are exercises in moral reasoning directed at the life
of a particular person or thing. Aphthonius suggests that the excellen-
cies and detractions of virtually any person or thing can be composed,
but the emphasis is on the clear delineation between the presence and
effects of good and evil.

The format is strict, and it bears on the comprehensive consideration of a person's life:

a. The exordium or introduction should include a statement of the
matter at hand, including the criteria by which the character will be
judged.

b. The person's heritage should be examined: does the person hail
from a land with a particular reputation, is his family reputable, what
influences upon his early life likely contributed to his thinking and
behavior later on?

c. The person's education is considered, especially his own talents
and habits (e.g., did the person take full advantage of his education?).

d. Most importantly, achievements are cataloged, then lauded or
condemned. Aphthonius requires that a man's spiritual and physical
attributes be considered, as well as his fortune (i.e., the providential
course of his life, including wealth, success, opportunity, etc.).

e. A comparison to another character of similar repute is suggested in order to further categorize the figure (e.g., President Bush's comparison of Saddam Hussein to Adolf Hitler prior to the Persian Gulf War).

f. Aphthonius prescribes a solemn epilogue, but for the modern student an upbeat application or an exhortation to imitate the person being praised might be equally appropriate.

From the Christian perspective, praise and blame exercises provide the student with an excellent opportunity to practice moral reasoning. To describe the habits of a person over his or her lifetime and then to compare them to authoritative ethical criteria is a valuable skill and one that teachers concerned with character development need to cultivate carefully. Several opportunities present themselves:

a. The opportunity to teach or to reinforce objective moral criteria (e.g., the cardinal sins or virtues; the Ten Commandments; institutional honor codes or codes of ethics).

b. The opportunity to help students understand the impact that actions have upon reputation and the importance of reputation to continuing success in life.

c. The opportunity to discourage self-righteousness and to encourage careful moral introspection as a dependable route to spiritual health.

The praise and blame exercises also provide for an expanded consideration of historical characters and events. Not only do ideas have consequences, but so do actions. Consider this: Oliver Cromwell is often regarded a hero of the English Reformation, but what effects has his Irish Policy had on the quality of life in Ireland today and the current conflict there? Does his treatment of the Irish color our consideration of whether Cromwell should be praised or censured for his achievements as ruler of England? A speech of praise or censure might help clarify the question for us.

Stylistic Exercises

These exercises provide the dialectical and stylistic flourishes that help ensure that speeches are both interesting and effective. In the modern context, they and exercises like them are commonly used to teach students how to write imaginative literature, especially short stories and novels. The rhetoric teacher who also teaches creative writing should resist the tendency to reduce rhetoric to style (*letteraturizzazione*) and should be careful to relegate these exercises to their proper place within the larger context of persuasive discourse. I especially recommend stylistic exercises for more experienced students or as occasional asides to invigorate the imagination of younger students. Either way, style requires careful attention to detail, which the student must learn over the course of his studies.[9]

6. COMPARISON

Comparison of characters is another dialectical exercise recommended by Aphthonius to heighten a student's awareness of the need for consistency in measuring the worth of people and things. Further, it requires that the student examine a more detailed aspect of each character than is necessary in praise or censure exercises. He encourages the novice orator to compare virtuous characters with characters possessing corresponding vices, all of which serves to increase the student's variety of diction, his consistency in argument, and his ability to present believable and interesting characters for consideration.

7. CHARACTERIZATION

Characterization is an imaginative tool somewhat related to the orator's responsibility in invention. The goal is to impersonate the emotional and moral state of a mythical or historical character by inventing a speech that the character might have uttered (e.g., Hecuba's thoughts as Troy is being sacked or Achilles' supposed words over Patroclus as he decides to reenter the battle for Troy). Creatively, it allows the student to attempt to inhabit another character, while it aids the ability to see another point of view as arguments are formed for use in persuasive discourse.

Advanced Rhetoric

Aphthonius completes his list of exercises with the categories thesis and proposal of law. In any comprehensive rhetoric program, students should progress to being able to compose a serious and lengthy argument based on solid research and to proposing some helpful course of action to their readers. While not really exercises in and of themselves, the abilities to propose and defend a thesis and to propose useful public policy (though not necessarily formally legal) is the natural culmination of a sound rhetorical pedagogy. The persuasive effect that well-trained orators can have on a culture will not be felt until they are able to perform competently in public discourse on matters of importance to a broader audience than themselves.

If a collection of good men and women speaking well is the most valuable commodity a culture can possess, then our schools must establish eloquence as the goal for every student. As it is, rarely do we coordinate the way students learn and the ways in which they will perform as leaders. Rarely do we connect the things we teach them every day with their responsibilities to seek the greater good and to draw their friends and neighbors after them. How will our students use language to benefit their neighbors? Will words and the ideas embodied in them come easily, or will our students simply be good men and women, possessing discernment but without the capacity to benefit those around them through appropriate speech and noble deeds?

nine

TEACHERS AND THE
LIBERAL ARTS TRADITION

SUCCESSFUL IMPLEMENTATION of a liberal arts curriculum requires faculty who are invested in the tradition and who can envision the benefits for themselves and for their students. The more familiar we teachers are with these disciplines, the more capable we are of teaching in ways that promote the goals of wisdom and eloquence. Still, despite the attractiveness of the proposal, adopting new and unfamiliar perspectives on our vocation is an intimidating prospect. Most of us require instruction in the literature of the tradition or in the liberal arts themselves—we know that we have engaged a tremendous personal and professional challenge.

One of the most common questions we answer is, "What kind of teacher is best qualified to teach in the Christian school committed to the liberal arts?" Over the years we have hired dozens of teachers and trained and evaluated dozens more. We are convinced that teaching is an artistic gift that some people possess and that some do not. For those with the aptitude to succeed in this noble profession, education and training can transform mediocrity into excellence. For those who do not have the aptitude, the same education and training may only serve to convince them to take up another craft.

THE PERSONAL CHALLENGE

Let us say this clearly: If you are a gifted teacher, teaching authentically in the liberal arts tradition is a totally accessible goal. It merely requires applying your giftedness to tasks that strengthen the students' sense of belonging to the Christian liberal arts tradition and a willingness to take personal responsibility for it. Good teaching is good teaching, regardless of the goals of the curriculum, and good teachers often find that teaching in a Christian school that values the liberal arts is the most satisfying move of their careers. Even though what follows might sound unachievable, keep in mind what Quintilian said two millennia ago about similar goals that he laid out for teachers and students:

> If any of my readers regards me as somewhat exacting in my demands, I would ask him to reflect that it is no easy task to create a [cultural leader], even though his education be carried out under the most favourable circumstances. . . . Therefore the rules which we lay down must be of the best.[1]

We are dealing in ideals because our goals for the education we offer extend beyond our classrooms into a culture that desperately needs the wise and eloquent students we produce. Based on the ways that most of us were taught in school and the ways that many of us were trained as professional teachers, moving into the liberal arts environment will require adjustments to our thinking and the application of our skills. And there is no such thing as instantaneous change. The changes will happen as we accept the necessity for change, wherever it exists in us, and as we develop conscious patterns of thinking about ourselves and our profession—habits of mind and heart.

HABITS OF THE MIND

We mentioned in the first chapter that the liberal arts tradition has been usurped by a progressive, secular insurgency in educational theories stemming back to the Enlightenment and finding an energizing American voice in the early twentieth century. The job of teaching and our role as teachers in students' lives has been damaged by this revolution. It is worth considering how the liberal arts tradition has been usurped in at least four areas that affect us every day: the place of the mind, the inheritance of wisdom, the importance of transcendent ideas, and scholarship.

First, despite all of the attention given to a student's spiritual and moral well-being, the liberal arts oriented teacher understands that her first job is to cultivate minds. We are, after all, teachers, and the mind is indispensable to learning. Even if one proposes a highly experiential type of teaching and learning, the mind is the repository for the memory of each experience that makes up the student's education. The liberal arts orientation places a high degree of confidence in each student's mind. Despite differences in aptitude, each student has innate capacity to remember, to analyze, and to synthesize information and experiences. The ideal liberal arts education does everything possible to maximize these intellectual abilities, producing students who possess the capacity to learn and to adapt what they have learned to all sorts of circumstances and challenges.

David Perkins summarizes the academic enterprise by saying bluntly, "Learning is a consequence of thinking."[2] Teachers who think well and who constantly attend to their students' habits of mind are laying invaluable groundwork for lifelong learning, irrespective of the context. Discipleship and spiritual formation are learning exercises that require thoughtfulness no less than mathematics. Athletics, fine arts, student organizations—every meaningful activity requires our minds to be engaged, and teachers who grasp this can use every circumstance to cultivate thoughtfulness. But the key component to the cultivation of minds is the curriculum and its learning goals.

While progressive schools have obviously not abandoned students' minds altogether, it is easy to wonder, sometimes, whether students' minds are first priority. "Socializing individuals" is one phrase that has come to represent much of progressive education. In the early parts of the twentieth century, the phrase had primarily to do with establishing a vocational track for each student. In the latter twentieth century, the focus drifted from economic socialization to psychological and relational priorities. Take, for instance, the four characteristics of an educated person, as described by the Alfred Adler Institute:[3]

1. Developing a positive attitude toward the self.
2. Developing a positive attitude toward difficulties.
3. Developing a positive attitude toward others.
4. Developing a positive attitude toward the other sex.

One would be hard-pressed to argue that these four attitudes should not result from a thoroughly Christian education, but it would be possible for a Christian teacher to nurture these attitudes and never help his students to achieve one useful thing academically.

Second, the liberal arts tradition requires that its practitioners learn from those who preceded them in the tradition, those who crafted it by their insight, creativity, and achievements. It is an inherited tradition of wisdom. The effects of this perspective on teachers are profound. We understand ourselves to be keepers of the tradition. It is our job to love the inherited tradition and to love the wisdom that it contains. To learn to love it, we must immerse ourselves in it.

The place to start for most of us is with the first three of the liberal arts themselves—grammar, dialectic, and rhetoric. The blind cannot lead the blind—we'll all end up in a ditch. Learning how to teach a third-grade grammar curriculum does not qualify a teacher as a grammarian. To teach grammar properly, one must know and understand grammar from the inside out, in a manner that is substantially more sophisticated and practiced than that of one's students.

As we noted previously, the most effective way to teach the elements of the *trivium* to students is in overlapping fashion. Once students have learned to read and write, they begin to study grammar, learning parts of speech, etc. By the time they are expertly analyzing any sentence put before them, they have begun their forays into formal logic, perhaps by studying the scientific method and inductive reasoning or informal fallacies. The start of their formal rhetorical training coincides closely with the point at which they gain facility with deduction and more abstract forms of reasoning.[4] The integrative nature of our instruction highlights the need to academically qualify teachers in the liberal arts according to the school's expectation for the students—at a bare minimum.

Ideally, teachers should be working through a measured, purposeful study of all three language arts, so that they each have a more accurate picture of the goal toward which their students are headed. The more each teacher knows about grammar, dialectic, and rhetoric, the more natural the liberal arts environment will feel to each student. When students open their first logic textbook in seventh grade, they should not be encountering a whole new universe of ideas. That is because their sixth and fifth and fourth grade teachers instinctively pointed them in the direction of formalized, orderly thinking at every opportunity.

In addition to the academic commitment to the tradition, Christian teachers have the opportunity in the liberal arts environment to point students to the dependable sources of wisdom that have been tested over millennia and have produced tremendous spiritual and cultural progress. Modern schools often model for their students the responsibility to invent individual meaning in every circumstance. Rejecting traditional authoritative sources, especially the Scriptures, they evaluate the prudence of thoughts and behavior solely from the results. "Did telling the truth get me what I wanted in this situation? If it did, then it must have been the right thing to do. If not, next time we'll reevaluate the importance of telling the truth." Teachers often burden students with the responsibility to devise their own literary, philosophical, and moral interpretive frameworks, on the assumed premise that the past cannot be trusted to help us understand our times.

But we are our tradition's conduits. It passes through us into the minds and habits of our students. So we work at modeling all that is best in the tradition, and we say to our students, "Follow me because I am being shaped by the wisdom of this great tradition, and you can be too!"

Accompanying this principle is a third premise—the centrality of ideas to the Christian educator's goals in the classroom. If education is truly a preparation for life, then all of the most important ideas that determine the quality of our lives must be discussed regularly. We must not waste our students' time with irrelevant trivia. The Christian classroom should resound with conversations and questions about faith, hope, and love. Truth, goodness, and beauty should find expression in every aspect of the curriculum. And we teachers should be constantly expanding our vocabulary and the breadth of our perspective on the most important questions of being human. "The one deep thought we had while reading *The Catcher in the Rye* our sophomore year of college" is not sufficient to support a career of leading young minds to contemplate life's great mysteries. We are leading them into "the conversation of the ages," and we teach by allowing them to see us already engaged in the dialogue.

The first condition for this conversation, and we cannot repeat this enough, is the assumption that truth and goodness and beauty are objective values that can be discovered. Relativism reduces conversation about transcendent ideas to the level of parlor games, and it minimizes the importance of genuine disagreements. Getting to know our students will usually result in the discovery that their thinking has largely been shaped by the relativistic spirits of the age, and they must be given the opportunity to rebel. Students cannot be forced to accept the existence of absolute values, but as teachers, we ought to constantly push them to confront the question and to engage one another and the great wealth of ideas we expose them to as if these things really matter.

In many schools, the conversation of the ages died ages ago, even before relativism set in. Pragmatism can destroy transcendent contemplation just as well, and it is often easier to justify. After all, what good is being able to talk about the problem of evil or divine ordination and human will if one can't support one's family? Preparation for life and preparation for the economy have been positioned as mortal enemies in many schools and in the minds of the teachers who support the schools' agendas for their students. In Louis Auchincloss's novel about an old boarding school headmaster, he has the retiring educator and ordained minister complain that the school trains its students to be philosophers and thinkers, but somehow they all end up stockbrokers.[5] The world needs thoughtful, Christian stockbrokers, but the schools that educate them as children must commit themselves to expanding their horizons beyond the material.

Even rigorous curricula can work against the need for ideas to characterize our interaction with our students if a "facts only" approach to teaching and assessing is allowed to take hold. Well-intentioned reformers who have grown sick of fact-less conventional curricula have recently revised state testing requirements to test a student's ability to recite specific facts as if preparing for their next *Jeopardy!* appearance. That many prominent schools in America can't be defined as "quality" even by that standard is a tragedy. But the tragic situation of our schools ultimately stems from a lack of insistence that students be required to think about important things, that they be held to high standards in synthesizing and expressing their ideas, and that the teachers who are most skilled at facilitating the conversation of the ages are rewarded for their efforts.

In short, our own minds must be trained by the consideration of truth, goodness, and beauty as overriding priorities in every academic pursuit. Our job is to constantly help our students connect the ordinary and seemingly mundane to the sublime and transcendent values that define the meaning of our existence. We only inspire our students to recognize and pursue truth, goodness, and beauty to the extent that we pursue them ourselves. As we encourage this pursuit, we transpose ourselves from "inheritors" of the liberal arts tradition into "transmitters," and we begin the same process of transformation in our students.

The fourth area to discuss can be touchy because many of us who teach at the grade-school level do not see ourselves as scholars. So, when someone makes the claim that one of the problems with our schools is that teachers are not often required to demonstrate scholarly aptitude, we hear them criticizing our intelligence or, worse, our commitment to education. But this tradition we advocate requires that teachers cultivate minds, assuming that their own minds have been properly cultivated. We are asking that teachers who represent the liberal arts tradition serve as keepers, interpreters, and conduits, modeling all that is best in our culture's past and present with the objective of preserving it for the future. We are looking for men and women for whom transcendent ideas and their historical consequences are a high priority. We are looking for a prototype that existed in days gone by, for "Renaissance people"—i.e., people with scholarly aptitude.

This does not mean that second grade teachers are best qualified for their positions by holding Ph.D.s, but it certainly does mean that second grade teachers should not be satisfied with an elementary intellect in themselves. Effective teachers are eminently practical. We must possess a firm grasp of known facts, which means that we can never stop learning about the things we teach. We must model the kind of clear, dependable thinking that our students so desperately need. Mental laziness in the forms of unfounded bias, sentimentalism, or presumption has no place in the liberal arts classroom. And in the end we provide our students with models for both the winsomeness and the scholarly prowess that they will need to lead the culture.

The extent to which teachers do not currently see this in themselves or express it in their classrooms should not be blamed on the teachers. The teacher who does not have the intelligence or the personal discipline to model scholarship for his or her students of any age is rare. We wouldn't be in this profession if we didn't want to use our brains every day! But the schools for which we work and the families we serve expect us to continue to grow, to expand our knowledge of the things we teach and even the things that just make us curious. Teachers should be given opportunities to study and to teach other teachers or parents. Teachers should be asked to write their thoughts about the things they teach and the kids to whom they teach them for the benefit of others.

While many teachers in conventional schools are well-educated and intellectually motivated, progressive schools, on the whole, reward professional credentials, government certification, and aptitude for socialization over scholarship. But most professional education credentials say little about competency in the subjects being taught or about the ability to cultivate minds. Instead, they reward and certify on the basis of psychosocial priorities. Thoughtfulness is not nearly as valuable in most schools as is organization, and the students who cannot conform to the organizational routines often find themselves "left behind" despite their intellectual gifts.

If we have been educated as professional teachers, chances are that our training focused a great deal on the social dynamics of our classrooms and spent little time, proportionally, deepening our understanding of the subjects we are called upon to teach. We find ourselves technically proficient and academically limited. If, on the other hand, we have been educated primarily in the liberal arts or sciences, then we enter the classroom with only our wits and our own experience of being taught. In either instance, we are ill-prepared to embody this great tradition, and we must covenant with our fellows to collectively bring ourselves up to snuff. We must always be aware that when we don't know what to do, we do what we know, and that will likely not be enough in this endeavor.

Schools that recognize this fact must accept the responsibility to educate and reeducate their faculties. Teachers who do not possess the basic aptitude and motivation described above cannot succeed, but those who are willing to transition from being mere committed professionals to being exceptional examples of the liberal arts tradition will have the time of their professional lives! The responsibility of administrators and educational leaders is to facilitate and reward those who are willing to take up the challenge.

HABITS OF THE HEART

One cannot build a Christian school without Christian faculty. A non-Christian teacher's presuppositions, no matter how sympathetic toward or accepting he may be of Christian ethics, places him at odds with the Christian worldview, especially in metaphysics (one's understanding of why and how things exist) and epistemology (one's understanding of how we can know what we know). This is an unacceptable conflict that renders the Christian school's mission ineffective and hypocritical. So, Christ must be the central reference point of the teacher's life in a way that recognizes him as the active and irresistible Creator, Ruler, and Redeemer of the universe.

The Christian teacher must also be committed to placing the welfare of others ahead of his own. Schools are relationally intensive environments in which pettiness and peevishness can have a highly destructive effect on everything that happens. Teachers, however, because of the thoughtfulness and conviction required by the profession, tend to think well and to hold their opinions forcefully. We are used to a high degree of autonomy in our classrooms, and we need to be trusted to do our jobs as we see fit. Strong thinking and strongly held convictions, without consideration of the need for harmony, is a relational and professional disaster in the making.

We agree with Gilbert Highet, Columbia University's eminent (and lonely) educational traditionalist, when he said that the most important quality a teacher possesses is kindness. The teacher who has the habits of mind and heart noted above and who can readily lay aside his own agenda and convenience for the sake of his students will be loved and admired by students, colleagues, administrators, and parents alike. The unnatural skill that must be developed in each teacher is to overlay clear standards of excellence with general kindliness and sincerity. Often the kindest thing a teacher can do for a child is to allow him to fail. But the teacher or school that allows children to fail just to prove a point or to add to their own sense of exacting standards lacks the humility that a Christian community of faith and learning must insist upon.

To illustrate the balancing act this point requires, here is a poetic admonition we have shared with our teachers from time to time:

- A well-planned course of study typically lends the greatest benefit to both students and teachers.

- Every expectation we place upon our students requires a corresponding effort from us, their teachers.

- Sometimes students fail.

- Failure is not the end of the world, but it needs to be remembered as a failure.

- Grades are indispensable assessments of a student's success.

- Sometimes we learn the most when we achieve the least.

- He still gets the "F."

- Teachers ought to feel every "F" as their own failure.

- Every good teacher wants each student to live up to his potential.

- They rarely do.

- Neither do we.

- True learning is a struggle, because it is against our natures.

- Good teachers, like primitive explorers, understand that they struggle against and want to dominate nature.

- We have not done our jobs if we have not induced our students to learn!

- There is no greater joy than to impart truth and to see it accepted into a student's heart.

If we are going to learn to love our students, we have to learn about them. We will certainly get to know the personalities assigned to our classrooms, but we also need to know about them generally. Aristotle spent a great deal of time trying to apply his rudimentary psychological observations to teaching and learning. Likewise, for the Christian liberal arts teacher, a basic, well-informed knowledge of areas of study such as developmental psychology, educational psychology, and brain research can help teachers avoid all sorts of silly, counterproductive mistakes. The worst situation a teacher can find himself in is to be constantly surprised that second graders sometimes don't make it to the bathroom or that seventh grade girls sometimes cry for seemingly no reason or that tenth grade boys instinctively compete with their male teachers for dominance in social situations.

We do acknowledge that we live in an overanalyzed, therapeutic society permeated by naturalistic presuppositions. That said, however, we commend Augustine once again,[6] and we encourage teachers who would really know and love their students to sift through the piles of psychological debris occasionally in search of the "Egyptian gold" that can still be found there. We must work at understanding our students' psychological tendencies, as these will influence many of their mental and intellectual endeavors. So we can rely on twenty years of trial and error, or we can expedite the learning curve by learning from those who have done solid, dependable research and were kind enough to record their observations.

Another aspect of knowing our students requires that we study their social habits. A colleague who heads a Christian upper school subscribes to magazines like *Cosmo Girl*, *Seventeen*, and *Dirt Bike* and displays them in the faculty lounge. The more we know about the moral norms, the materialistic expectations, the social posturing that students are learning from the culture, the better equipped we are to teach and disciple *them* rather than just some idealized group of students that doesn't actually exist.

Developing these habits is not a simple challenge, either for teachers or for their schools. Doing so constitutes, however, the only reasonable way to expect the values of the Christian liberal arts tradition to permeate our students' experience in school. Their fashioning as wise and eloquent cultural leaders depends upon it.

ten

LEARNING AND THE
LIBERAL ARTS TRADITION

WE BELIEVE STRONGLY that the liberal arts provide Christian educators and their students with a dependable structure for the pursuit of wisdom and eloquence—both of which are in short supply in our current culture. At the same time, we also acknowledge that the tradition poses some unique challenges for teachers, especially given many of the expectations we have developed in our profession. First, the liberal arts provide a general approach to schooling, but in many instances, and in most disciplines, history is somewhat lacking in precise guidance as to how these general ends might be achieved or assessed—especially in a modern context. Second, the tradition has much to say about broad areas of content and describes the general outcomes for our students, but the historical record generally does not prescribe a specific pedagogical method suitable to achieving these ends. To a great extent, it falls to talented teachers who are committed to the ends of wisdom and eloquence and the general means of the liberal arts to construct a specific pedagogical paradigm consistent with our goals.

Keep in mind that the *trivium* is not a pedagogical method. In some recent expositions of the *trivium*, for example, memory as a mode of instruction has been associated with "grammar" as if it were a "grammatical" style of teaching. Taking this to its ultimate end, as some have, we might conclude that once a student has moved from learning "grammar" every day to learning logic, he no longer needs to commit anything to memory. Of course, this is not the case, especially in the modern curriculum in which new disciplines of study are introduced throughout the student's career, even into graduate school.

Similarly, a "rhetorical" style of teaching cannot be reserved for older students, who must be introduced to principles of rhetoric from the earliest ages. We might assign Socratic instructional methodology to a "dialectical" stage of instruction (as it is, literally, a form of dialectic), but we know from experience that Socratic teaching is both possible and necessary at any stage of a student's development. Neither would Socrates himself (nor Aristotle, Cicero, Quintilian, or Augustine) have recognized the highly structured medieval forms from which we derive much of what we know about how the liberal arts work.

Two basic facts about the liberal arts are worth reiterating: (1) they comprise a set of linguistic and mathematical subjects designed to produce wisdom and eloquence as their chief benefit, and (2) they inform the outcomes for skills and content in our schools, while leaving us to figure out how best to achieve those outcomes. It is a series of content and skills that requires a great deal of ingenuity to help each element seem alive and relevant to students. Further, as we have already learned from our examples from antiquity, the content and skills of the *trivium* need not be fully mastered before embarking upon the mathematical content and skills of the *quadrivium*. The two broad areas of liberal arts learning must, instead, be tackled simultaneously and incrementally so that the knowledge and skills of each discipline build upon those of the others.

However, we do believe, as did the ancients and medievalists, that the first essential component of learning is "remembering" and that the essence of effective teaching is helping students, at every level of cognitive development, to remember critical content and skills and how to apply them. We also believe that effective methods for helping students remember will change as their cognition changes or develops.

Beyond remembering, there is thinking! The most important statement in Dorothy Sayers's speech on the *trivium* was: "although we succeed in teaching our pupils 'subjects,' we fail lamentably on the whole in teaching them how to think."[1] Is it possible to have taught "subjects" well, if the product of our instruction in science or history, for example, is not sound thinking about the discipline? David Perkins describes the successful school as a virtual laboratory for "thoughtful learning" that puts thinking at the center of everything that happens in the classroom. "We need schools that are full of thought, schools that focus not just on schooling memories but on schooling minds."[2] Perkins describes the crisis of modern American education simply. "The bottom line is that we are not getting the retention, understanding, and active use of knowledge that we want." In short, in all that we are requiring students to remember (when we are courageous enough to require students to remember), we have a hard time teaching them to think.

MODES OF TEACHING AND LEARNING

Just two short decades ago, independent schools along with most colleges and universities believed their missions to be fulfilled if high-quality faculty were hired and simply allowed to shut the doors of their classrooms and *teach*. Since that time, growing educational consumerism and political activism over educational quality have led to at least two paradigm shifts that have combined to move the educational emphasis strongly in the direction of *student learning*.

First, regional and professional accrediting bodies found themselves pressured to change their accountability focus from emphases upon *inputs* (such as faculty credentials, numbers of library volumes, and classroom "seat time") toward measurable *outcomes* (such as departmental and whole-instituition standards of learning, benchmarking against other institutions' best practices, satisfaction surveys, and external standardized measures of learning). "Assessment" became the means by which accrediting agencies held institutions accountable as they, in turn, were held accountable to drive assessment by government agencies and citizen boards and councils.

Second, as colleges and schools struggled with the notion of assessment for assessment's sake, the sound business principle of Continuous Quality Improvement began to emerge as the logical end of educational assessment. With this development, the reams of data that institutions were expected to gather about themselves found a higher purpose than that of simply demonstrating to outsiders that data were being gathered—namely, ever improving educational services and, chief among them, student learning.

Despite years of resistance, the principles of measuring outcomes as opposed to inputs and the routine gathering of information and data for the express purpose of improving educational services are here to stay.

There is simply no room in today's "educational market" for the old-style autonomous, thoroughly independent faculty. Schools are becoming organic units, and faculty must work together with other school stakeholders (boards, parents, and even students) to ensure that students are learning what mission-driven outcomes indicate that they should. In short, effective teaching these days means helping students learn.

We know from experience and from myriad studies on learning and cognition that whether we are teaching in fifth-century B.C. Greece or in twenty-first century A.D. America, there are still only a handful of ways in which students learn *and* learn to think about what they are learning. More elaborate theories may subdivide these into more complex taxonomies, but we will focus on three primary ways in which students learn. We are most comfortable expressing them as Adler did:[3] (1) acquisition of new knowledge, (2) critical interaction, and (3) meaningful expression. We believe they correspond somewhat closely with Plato's progression of sensory, intellectual, and intuitive learning. Whatever we call them, the master teacher understands how to apply each step in order to help any group of students learn in virtually any circumstance.

ACQUIRING NEW KNOWLEDGE

In recent generations, "rote memory" has been roundly criticized as a mode of learning, even to the point that it is not uncommon to hear claims that "learning by rote is not learning at all." To the extent that "memorizing" is viewed as an individual exercise of attempting to force uncontextualized information into short-term memory, we agree with these critics. Such exercises notoriously result in forgetting information as quickly as it is gained. Without the basic acquisition and retention of new information, however, real learning simply cannot occur. Perkins and the team working on Harvard Project Zero concluded that "students emerge from primary, secondary, and even college education with remarkable gaps in basic background knowledge about the world they live in. A case in point: Most seventeen-year-olds cannot identify the date of the U.S. Civil War within half a century."[4]

Responding to this crisis in basic knowledge, influential educators here and there have awakened to the disastrous consequences of educational programs that don't require students to remember anything.

Traditionalists like E. D. Hirsch and his Cultural Literacy curriculum have reinserted "remembering" as a basic requirement of a well-rounded education.[5] While strictly subject-oriented instruction and assessment cannot serve as an exclusive approach that teaches students to think about and apply what they know, it is certainly preferred over prevalent alternatives of vacuous, factless curriculum programs.

There was a time, prior to the invention of the printing press, when it was possible for one person to read every published word. Conceivably, if one could read everything that was then known, one could also remember it. Those days are long gone, and as human knowledge and interests increase at the exponential rates we are witnessing right now, educators are faced with the dilemma of how much to commit to memory. If we cannot know everything, and if we have such ready access through technology to just about everything we might need to know, why memorize at all? With the Internet at our fingertips, Einstein's famous quote about not memorizing anything he could find in a book seems even more relevant than when he first said it. Understanding further that he made this comment as an adult whose cognition had matured beyond that with which we are primarily concerned puts his idea into even better perspective. We must also acknowledge that Einstein remembered what was essential to the great intellectual feats he accomplished.

But we need to say it again for our times: memory is indispensable to learning, and there is no practical definition of learning that does not presuppose that students must remember things. In an educational environment in which this position is not to be taken for granted, we have to work to perfect this aspect of our instruction.

If you are younger than fifty years old, and if you did not attend a traditional private school or labor under a stubborn, old public school principal, you were likely not required to remember much as a child. The proliferation of self-help books on memory skills for adults is evidence enough that a vital piece of ordinary education has collapsed. So when most of us set about to help our students remember things we've taught them, we are already working without a clear model of how it should be done.

A lot has been learned about memory in recent years. Not long ago, memory was understood to be a singular skill. There were people with good memories and people with bad ones. Good memories could be increased and sharpened; people with bad memories were considered very difficult, if not impossible to educate. "Brain research" has expanded our understanding considerably. We now know that there are short-term and long-term varieties of memory, semantic and episodic memories, and motor and linguistic forms of memory.[6] Each of these discoveries expands the potential for the use of memory in teaching and learning, and every teacher ought to have a general and dependable understanding of our rapidly developing knowledge about how people remember.

Keep in mind, the genius of liberal arts teaching is its correlation to universal modes of learning, memory being the first and most obvious to consider. For example, learning to think like a grammarian depends heavily upon memory and is supported by an encyclopedic knowledge of the elements of language. Teaching the basics of grammar or any other discipline at a young age is easier, as Sayers noted, because young children's minds are like sponges. They are made to absorb information of all kinds, expanding more and more as the full shapes of their minds are realized.

The master teacher knows that this is an opportunity that must be exploited. Whenever a student presents herself willing and able to learn, whether developmentally or attitudinally, the alert teacher must be poised to take full advantage. So, when those five-, six-, and seven-year-olds with their absorbent minds meander into our classrooms, we teachers must be ready with the appropriate information and methods to fill their minds. As Hugo of St. Victor observed, the information learned may be less important in itself than it is to easing later learning.

APPROPRIATE INFORMATION

So what should be remembered? Each school must determine its own priorities, remembering that the information selected for memory at the earliest stages of the curriculum provides students with a structural framework for all future learning. We must look first to the desired end of the educational process, to the skills, knowledge, and virtues we want to be universally inherent in our graduates and determine how to get them there. The tenth-grade curriculum is preparatory for the twelfth, the seventh for the tenth, right down to the K or pre-K level. This forward-looking perspective keeps entry-level learning from becoming frivolous or provincial. For example, it may be cute for first graders to learn a song in Chinese or to learn to count to twenty in Swahili, but if neither of those exercises prepares them for some future related aspect of the curriculum, it is of lesser value.

Schools that value memory as a priority in the younger years face two temptations. First, schools will be tempted to require nothing more from students than memory because it is relatively easy to teach and to assess. Second, schools will be tempted to require students to memorize information without considering that information's future relevance because it impresses parents and projects an ethic of purposeful use of classroom time. The first temptation is addressed by including incremental elements of dialectical and rhetorical skills in our teaching and learning objectives, but the second should be discussed here.

One unfortunate social reality that many educators embrace and use as their basis for much-needed affirmation is that many parents are too easily impressed by the quality of education their children receive. Traditionalists often accuse progressivists of taking advantage of parent gullibility by throwing creative projects at the students and parents, without regard to content. While many parents secretly resent the amount of time spent in the typical elementary or middle school on these projects, they are also easily convinced that projects represent a clear demonstration of learning. If a child can generate a multimedia report or an imaginative display of information, it must mean that he knows and understands the topic.

The same gullibility can be preyed upon by demonstrations of memory. A traditional school can prop its students up in a PTA meeting and have them recite reams of material, from the Declaration of Independence to passages from the Bible to Latin endings. The parents are impressed and pleased, as most of us are anytime our children do something successfully in public, and the teachers can relax, having been affirmed that training the children to recite information, no matter how relevant, passes as quality education. In truth, such public experiences are important to liberal arts learning since they provide occasion for rhetorical development, but the relevance of the exercise to the curriculum and to future learning is essential for the school that wishes to reach beyond trivial displays.

So, the choice of what should be remembered by students depends largely on the framework of the overall curriculum and the role that any specific exercise plays in the overall objectives for each student. Schools with a strong Eurocentric or Western culture emphasis would do well to consult Hirsch's criteria[7] for cultural literacy or programs designed with liberal arts learning specifically in mind. Schools that require a certain level of proficiency in a foreign language might start integrating vocabulary and grammatical forms before the language is taught formally. Math "facts" such as multiplication tables and conversions are essential to higher functioning in mathematics, especially for typical students who will struggle with abstract concepts and don't need to be distracted by computational errors.

Many liberal arts oriented schools are skilled at designing dramatic and effective memory aids to their humanities programs,[8] but math and science education requires the same attention to detail and to a cumulative program of memory. Arithmetic skill is largely a function of memory, as is the application of math to science in conversions and other fundamental skills. The mnemonic foundation for this essential information should be laid early and often if we expect students to consistently excel in math and science.

English language, classical language, and modern foreign language programs that place a proper emphasis on grammar should have clearly articulated memory components, so students can be reminded, year after year, of the same rules and structures, especially as they make the transition from grammar-based to composition- or translation-based instruction.

SENSORY MODES OF REMEMBERING

Ancient educators understood intuitively what educational psychology and brain research have confirmed empirically: memory is accessed and reinforced by sensory experiences. When students can associate new information with what they see, hear, feel, and even taste and smell at the time, the incorporation of that information into long-term memory is greatly enhanced.

Educational psychologists are fairly unified in their acceptance of what are often called "modalities" of learning. It is generally believed that people have a predisposition to being auditory, visual, or kinesthetic learners. For the conscientious teacher, this reality poses two responsibilities.

The first is to design pedagogy that takes into account the various learning styles of one's students. If instruction centers, as it too typically does in the college classroom, strictly on lecturing to the students, the auditory learner will engage the material. At the same time, the visual and kinesthetic learners will experience disconnect and boredom—which for young students may result in behavior that disrupts the learning of others. Lessons that are approached multi-modally, incorporating visual, auditory, and kinesthetic activities, give students the benefit of multi-sensory stimulation in committing information to memory and reinforce memory for a broad range of students. Mnemonic associations can be created between words or ideas and physical motions, as well as visual images. Teaching students to encounter information in a multi-sensory way can create further associations.

We have already seen an example of this in our description of an integrated approach to teaching reading, writing, spelling, and vocabulary. The student hears the word (external auditory), writes the word (external and internal kinesthetic), sees the word (external visual), says the word (internal auditory), and hears himself saying the word (external auditory). Four activities converge upon the mastery of the simple task. Similar examples may be drawn from and devised for any subject or lesson. In math, for example, children see and hear numbers or equations, write what they hear and see, and interact with physical aids (manipulatives) to experience numeric learning.

A multi-modal approach to teaching memory works whether the teacher grasps each child's individual learning style or not. Assessing individual learning styles, however, is a rather simple process, and individual instruction can be enhanced by casting instruction in a suitable modality for a given student. When helping a student who doesn't "get" the visual presentation of a lesson, it is a simple thing to recast the lesson in auditory or kinesthetic terms and a joy to see the "light" go on.

It is one thing to recognize a student's predisposition to a particular learning style. It is quite another, and far more critical to his future ability to learn effectively, to train him in his ability to learn through all his senses. It is a sad reality that the great bulk of college-level instruction is characterized by "the talking head" or "sage on the stage," and the student who is tethered to a visual or kinesthetic learning style has not become an independent learner. Teachers who address themselves to these principles of learning will be much better equipped to help every student become a genuine multi-modal learner.

With the foregoing principles in mind, we suggest that another key to helping students remember is modeling. Nothing reinforces learning for the young student more than repetition and corporate learning. Rehearsing math facts or poems or parts of speech together in class and using a variety of modalities in the process serves as a template for students to tackle and remember all kinds of information. This, of course, requires that teachers themselves be able to commit to memory what they will require of their students. But if you're intimidated by this prospect, the notion of collective memory in the classroom should be even more appealing!

The need for acquiring and remembering new information does not diminish with age. Rather, the effective means of helping students remember changes as they develop cognitively. If memory is an important component of our instruction in ninth grade, we must figure out a way for those ninth graders to remember and review the things that must be remembered together as a function of study skills objectives. The goals should be that when they are learning on their own, we can be sure that they are not spending inordinate amounts of time and energy and still not remembering what they need to. As an example, learning biochemical cycles and metabolic pathways such as the Krebs or Calvin cycles is an arduous task for most students. Lecturing on these topics will be of little help to a student's memory; yet knowing these cycles by heart is prerequisite to engaging the topics critically and analytically (e.g., determining the number of calories that must be consumed to sustain a particular metabolic function). The artistic visuals that characterize most modern texts are only a little more help in achieving these ends. Here the astute teacher will have students rehearse the cycles on the board or at least on paper at their desks, combining kinesthetic and visual modalities as they repeat the exercise until it can be achieved from memory. The multi-modal methods of gathering and applying information that are learned together in the classroom are repeated individually with highly effective results.

CRITICAL INTERACTION

As students mature in their cognitive development, they increasingly benefit in their remembering and in the ultimate goal of thoughtful learning by critical interaction with material. This critical interaction allows information to be used, analyzed, and experimented with, demonstrating both its usefulness to solve problems and the need to gain more information as applications become more complex. The application of critical interaction to mathematics or logic is quite obvious: an understanding of solving problems comes from solving increasingly complex problems, and lots of them. So adequate class time should be devoted to solving problems as a class and to working problems individually with guidance from teacher and peers: "Who can help Billy with #7?" "Who can work #12 on the board?"

The power of critical interaction for remembering whole "sense sections" from literature, history, or the Scriptures is perhaps less obvious. As a senior in college, I (Littlejohn) was privileged to teach a college Sunday school class at a large church. As we made our way together through a book of the New Testament, I would often cross-reference the passage to other passages of Scripture and would frequently have class members or visitors ask afterward, "what Scripture memory method do you use?" The assumption was that I employed a "topical memory" or similar system to commit isolated verses to memory. In reality, I wasn't actually "quoting" Scripture; at least not verbatim. The method I used to engage the Scriptures was critical interaction. I would focus on a manageable passage of Scripture and read it in as many versions as I could find and reflect upon it, off and on, for hours, if not days. Then I would analyze it using all the "helps" I could find, including studies in the original languages, to the best of my abilities. Finally, I would consider what applications I could draw from the passage to my life and to the world in which I lived. The inevitable result was that I could generally rehearse the gist of the passage in succinct order and recall with fair accuracy the chapter and verse for each portion of the text. Had anyone checked my word-for-word accuracy, he would have discovered that I was not "quoting" any known translation but was paraphrasing the essence of the passage from a memory gained through critical interaction. Some may disagree with my definition, but I have come to describe this process as "meditation," and I find it as effective for learning poetry, speeches, or historic documents as I do for the Scriptures.

In his *Paideia Proposal*, Mortimer Adler describes a sequence of teaching activities designed to facilitate critical interaction. A simple Latin lesson serves as an example of Adler's didactic, coaching, and Socratic approach to critical interaction.[9]

> Didactic: We have taught the students that when they see a noun ending in "m," it is likely an accusative singular. Accusative endings often indicate a direct object. To help them remember, we have added "m" endings to our noun declensions and repeated them orally together and individually. The goal is that they remember the ending when they encounter it in translation.
>
> Coaching: The students are given a list of sentences like *"Pueri lucam vident"* to translate. The teacher roams from desk to desk, overseeing the translations, asking each student to justify his or her translation of at least one sentence, correcting the student's assumptions when necessary (e.g., "Okay, I see what you're doing, but remember that even if 'lucam' could be the subject, it would have to agree in number with the verb. How does that change things for you?"). The goal is to ensure that each student is translating using a consistent method that avoids grammatical and syntactical mistakes.
>
> Socratic: An open question: "Using what we know, how else might we say this in Latin?" The goal is to begin to explore other possibilities for expressing an idea with greater economy or clarity.

We also see in this example how the language arts of grammar, dialectic, and rhetoric assist the process of critical interaction. Grammar requires that students both know the information and how to apply it— a logical skill that we can begin to teach to even young students in simple ways.[10] Memory by itself, however, cannot demonstrate the utility of the information the students have learned, and independent use of proper grammar in composition and editing will require that students be able to discern between stylistic options intuitively.

The second liberal art, dialectic, is designed to help students develop faculties of discernment based on regular patterns of thinking. The point is to bring predictability and order to the students' minds. It is no small thing to bring a student from the point of only being able to reflect on things outside of himself (like arithmetic problems, snails, or nouns) to being able to think about (analyze) his own thinking. And the only way to do it in a predictable and assessable fashion is to teach him logic.

Logic, like any other academic discipline, must be learned through a process of memory, critical interaction, and meaningful expression. There is a basic body of knowledge that must be gained didactically, and the utility of the information must be tested through coaching and Socratic interactions.

Each liberal arts discipline produces a set of transferable skills that increases a student's ability to learn other things. This, perhaps, is especially true of logic, which allows the student to engage all of his studies within a dialectical framework. The teacher's ability to solicit meaningful critical responses to subject matter increases dramatically by the predictability of the logic student and the accountability for disciplined thinking that logic provides. As students gain greater facility in formal logic, our instruction capitalizes on their increased sophistication. The more confident we are of the student's mastery of the objectives laid out in the logic curriculum, the more those objectives find their way into our instruction, further justifying the notion of a dialectically oriented curriculum.

Critical interaction and Socratic teaching that builds this way is more challenging to master, because it is related to a specific body of knowledge. A school may make its own list of the essential dialectical objectives, coordinating them to the nomenclature of its logic curriculum, but if the faculty has not mastered them and integrated each one into the objectives for every discipline, then an authentically dialectical environment cannot exist, and critical interaction suffers.

MEANINGFUL EXPRESSION

As we train our students to make both grammatical and logical use of language and the information they are acquiring in every other area of study, we are training them toward real eloquence. A brain full of organized information is a form of education, but it can just as easily tempt students and teachers to settle for a less-than-complete definition of teaching and learning. Remember, the "object of our quest"[11] is much more than the development of formidable *Jeopardy!* contestants. We are shaping students whose lives will exhibit true wisdom and eloquence.

Despite the trouble of learning logic so that we are at least keeping pace with our students' intellectual development, it is relatively easy, still, to teach students didactically and to coach them in the use of forms. To solicit meaningful expression on a regular basis is much harder, beginning with the task of defining what constitutes meaningful expression in our classes.

When we speak of this mode of instruction, we are describing activities that move students from remembering information and testing how well they remember that information in pre-set circumstances toward using what they have learned to solve problems, to connect information from one context to another, or to create a new framework for understanding or describing the world around them.

To begin, let's put aside some potential biases. First, as much as we value the uniqueness of each of our students, every contribution a student makes is not necessarily meaningful. Second, meaningful expression can be as much a valid objective for younger students as for older. Third, meaningful expression is possible and should be required in any discipline, even math.

Now, let's give ourselves a definitive framework within which we can judge the expressions our students offer. You might even put these, or some version of your own criteria, on the wall of your classroom to help students evaluate the quality of their own thoughts. Meaningful expression should:

1. Fit into the logical context of the topic at hand.
2. Instruct others who are considering the same topic.
3. Help to move the conversation toward reasonable conclusions.

Mortimer Adler suggests the goal of "enlarging understanding of ideas or values"[12] as the primary aspect to keep in mind as we seek our students' input regarding the things that we are learning together.

The temptation to resist in this mode of instruction is to create assignments or to ask questions that implicitly require a "correct" answer. It is not easy to introduce ambiguity into an assessment of a student's performance without creating a feeling of subjectivity. It is much simpler to check off "right" or "wrong" rather than to explore the process by which the student is attempting to "enlarge understanding of ideas or values." A well-developed Socratic method can help alleviate a teacher's tension by effectively limiting the range of discussion. A student's ability to limit himself to a specific problem or issue within a problem demonstrates discipline, which aids in developing intellectual maturity.

The ability to express oneself meaningfully is the basic foundation of rhetorical skill. The earlier and the more often we draw out our students' extended ideas on things they are learning, the better prepared they will be for the responsibility to lead the culture toward a common good. A common fault of many modern leaders is that they do not possess the discipline to speak consistently to the matters that people care about. "Staying on message" is more than a political campaign issue; it is a crucial ability for anyone who takes up the challenge of improving the lives of those around him or her.

Of course, meaningful expression is not taught and learned in Socratic classroom discussions exclusively. The other principal method of rhetorical expression is writing. Whether the assignment is a creative topical essay, a critique of a theatrical performance, or a laboratory report, students must be taught meaningful expression through writing. If writing is for reading, we will best serve our students as editors, encouraging individual style and voice while holding them accountable for good grammar, sound logic, and thoughtful applications of knowledge in everything they write.

appendix A

A MESSAGE TO PARENTS

IN THE LATE 1980s, while serving as a university professor, I (Littlejohn) grew increasingly concerned each year over how ill-prepared many of my students seemed for college-level work. As my own children approached school age, my wife and I didn't believe that we were equipped to teach our children at home, but we knew that we would likely have to personally supplement our children's formal educations if they were going to be prepared for college and for life.

Our suspicions were first confirmed when our son entered first grade in the local public school. As the only class member who had attended a private kindergarten, he had not learned the eighteen sight words his new classmates had memorized the previous year. All the class activities and games were based on these few words, and he was embarrassed that his classmates did well at these while he was clueless. He believed that he was the only kid in the class who could not read, and he was crushed by the experience.

When we talked to his teacher, we learned that none of the children could read. They just recognized these eighteen sight words, and home "reading" assignments were accompanied by a strict charge from the teacher not to venture beyond a certain page (lest parents stumble into new words and discover that their child was not reading). The teacher explained, as if she were speaking for the whole educational establishment, "We really don't know how children learn to read. It just happens." What we understood her to be actually acknowledging was of even greater concern and an ominous sign for our son—and, we suspected, for many children across the nation. This well-credentialed, state-certified teacher did not know how to teach children the skill of reading, and she had been convinced somehow that this was normal and that no one else knew either. It was entirely up to the child to discover the skill through exposure to various "reading-related" activities, cheerfully facilitated by well-meaning "teachers." My response was to buy a phonics book and teach my son to read. Soon, and for some time, he was the only student in class who really could read. But from grade one, we were already faced with supplementing his education! However, our ability to continue supplementing was soon lost as the onslaught of nightly "busywork" assignments began to increase. There was no time to complete school assignments *and* actually learn something from Mom and Dad at home.

Had we stumbled onto an isolated occurrence? Was our son's teacher the only first grade teacher who hadn't been trained to do the job of preparing her students for a literate life? Not by a long shot. Over many years of interviewing dozens of teachers I have never had a fresh college graduate volunteer to teach first grade. These candidates knew that first grade teachers in our schools would be expected to teach non-readers to read (a very measurable outcome), and they didn't know how. How could this be?

It turns out that colleges of education across our nation are short-changing our future elementary schoolteachers. University education courses survey various reading, writing, and math curricula and methodologies but rarely teach our future teachers how to actually teach "the three Rs." Teaching candidates have typically learned how to "facilitate discovery," how to encourage children to learn on their own, but not how to teach. Now, it is true that children can learn through independent discovery. When a child sticks her finger into an electrical socket, she discovers something on her own. But reading skills, writing skills, and basic mathematics skills cannot be discovered independently. Bright children do learn with the help of television learning programs, but in any case, they must be taught. Sadly, our nation's schools are filled with children who cannot perform these basic skills because teachers have not been taught how to teach them. In fact, most conventionally trained teachers who entered the field after the 1930s are completely ignorant of a definite pedagogy of literacy. Those who entered the field before the thirties are, of course, no longer teaching.

Let us hasten to say that the teachers are not to blame for this troubling state of affairs. Every teacher we have trained, every teacher who has acquired, either in-house or at our national conferences, the easily obtainable and (like bicycle riding) unforgettable skill of teaching children to read has been thrilled to teach reading. Further, it is common in our schools for every first grader (even those identified as possessing "specific learning disabilities") to read a magazine off the coffee table by Christmas.

I was surprised and amused when a Master's-trained reading specialist arrived at our school and asked to observe the first-grade classroom. After spending a day with the class, she came to my office in a very excited state. She explained that her own experience was that she could not read Dr. Seuss (not having previously memorized his nonsensical words) before learning in her Master's program the research-based methodology that she now employed with individual children to correct their reading deficiencies by teaching them to decode English words. Her excitement was in observing the success of the same methodologies applied to a class of twenty-four children at once. She was delighted and surprised to see how well the methods worked in a classroom setting.

As one who has educated students from kindergarten to college, I can assert that nothing in all of education gives greater satisfaction than seeing a child's world open before him as he learns to read. But teachers are being denied this joy by schools of education that have forgotten the wonder, even the necessity, of such things. But it is unfair even to lay blame at the feet of these educators who are themselves caught up in a decades-long stream of modernist thinking. Consider the experience I had while serving as academic vice president for an academically rigorous denominational college. I challenged our reading specialist to attend the workshop I was hosting to prepare teachers to use a research-based approach to teaching reading. I asked her to report back to me, giving me an objective assessment of the method from the perspective of her professional preparation. The professor was excited when she reported back that despite her initial (and understandable) skepticism, she had recognized that the approach thoroughly integrated a variety of techniques that she had taken years to gather into an eclectic approach and that the method she observed did it more effectively.

In the end, she became a strong proponent of such methods and has employed them as a personal ministry of faith in inner-city settings to open the world of literacy to urban children.

Of course, the crisis is not limited to the first grade or to the teaching of the "three Rs." Consider a study reported in the journal *Physics Today* in 1989. Comparing math performance among thirteen-year-olds in six countries, Korean children scored first, while American teens scored dead last. When asked how they felt about their math abilities, 67 percent of American children believed they were good in math, while 77 percent of the Koreans thought they were not good in math. This study and others like it have been widely criticized by conventional educators, but the lesson here is easily understood. It should be no surprise that American kids outperformed their competitors in the self-esteem department while being trounced in academics. The teachers who taught those kids their math were themselves trained in programs and by professors who emphasized the emotional comfort of children over rigorous intellectual exercise and accountability for knowledge. In reality, both are important, but nothing boosts the confidence of a child like genuine learning, and nothing is so satisfying to a young scholar as the actual mastery of essential learning skills.

Consider further the 1994 study reported by the Capital Research Center, which showed that only 32 percent of public high school seniors could "read proficiently." Thirty-one percent could not read even at "a basic level." Even more shocking, perhaps, was that less than half the seniors in private schools were proficient readers, and 16 percent of private-school students could barely read at all! This study too has been widely challenged, but we must still ask some difficult questions. How did things get so bad in our nation's education systems, and why are the private school students often performing little better than their public-school counterparts?

Let's take a look at some history. From ancient times, educators held that it was each generation's responsibility to pass along to the next the skills, knowledge, and virtues necessary to engage their culture intelligently and to be positive contributors to and leaders in society. Since the time of Christ, nothing has shaped human thought and culture more than Christianity and the Bible. However, with the dawn of the philosophical age known as the Enlightenment in the eighteenth century, a new way of thinking began to spread that would eventually lead both to the rejection of Christian influences on learning and (strangely enough) to uncertainty about the need to teach children a positive set of intellectual skills or an absolute core of cultural knowledge. Many current educators scoff at the notion of teaching children basic learning skills. Others laugh at their own colleagues who promote cultural literacy and the importance of teaching a common core of knowledge.[1]

Equally worrisome is the pervasive confusion about teaching values. Of the three (skills, knowledge and values), however, values confusion may be the most understandable. After all, in school systems serving a pluralistic society, whose values (if any) should be woven into the fabric of the curriculum? For patriotic Americans, it is a bit of a conundrum that our democratic political structure dictates that the values of the majority (or an activist minority) will be represented. Despite our commitment to democratic principles, it is a dangerous thing to have the quality of my child's education determined democratically.

Another significant contributor that affected these trends in American education is worth addressing here. With the rise of modernist thinking over the past several decades and the accompanying cultural elevation of science throughout our culture, science departments at our nation's universities began to flourish as government and foundation grants poured in for supporting grand experiments. Not wanting to be left out, "social scientists," including professors of education, soon began to engage in "scientific" experimentation so that they, too, could attract extramural funding for their departments. The effect has been cataclysmic for our nation's schools.

When a biologist experiments on guinea pigs, the "guinea pigs" are, in fact, guinea pigs. If the biology experiment "fails," you scrap it and start a new experiment with new guinea pigs. But when professional educators and graduate students in education (who are pressured to do something entirely new) conduct educational experiments, their "guinea pigs" are children, yours and mine. The unintended consequence of the educator's empirical approach is that when a widely supported educational experiment fails, a whole generation of children loses out on the education they could and should have had. Still, the colleges of education (and after them our nation's schools) move from one failed approach to the next, even abandoning the rare method that works in favor of the newest and latest educational fad.

Yet, this is only part of the story. It turns out that conventional schools don't really spend that much time educating children anyway. Most of the time is spent on *enculturation*. We visited this topic more thoroughly in chapter 3, but simply stated, enculturation is what naturally occurs in children while they are growing up. It comprises the influences of parents, teachers, pastors, peers, television, music, and video games, to name a few.

John Westerhoff, professor of theology and Christian nurture at Duke Divinity School, summarizes the situation well:

> In point of fact, schools may have become the most significant primary association in contemporary society. By the time children are 12 years of age, they have spent more hours in school than they have spent with their families and religious community combined. Indeed it would take 75 years of attending church and church school regularly to equal the school's influence in the first 12 formative years of a person's life. Further, schools are not solely instructional institutions in which reading, writing, and arithmetic are taught. Schools are fundamentally agents of enculturation. As Phillip Jackson notes, more than 90% of the time a child spends in school is spent on enculturation, while only 10% is spent on instruction. The hidden curriculum of the school [i.e., enculturation] is, it appears, more influential than the stated curriculum.[2]

It is frightening to realize that the educational establishment has stopped educating our children and has begun, instead, to instill in them values and notions about our culture and society that are often not our own. Worse still, our best teachers at schools, both public and private (like fish swimming against the current from a broken dam), are helpless to do anything substantive about it. Even if they could, it would take too long for any given child within the system to realize the benefit from it. The sad truth is that universal educational reform just doesn't work. Unless educators find a drastically different structural framework, a wholly distinct paradigm for education, there can be no lasting change. It is just such a paradigm (one that integrates genuine, historically proven, effective scholasticism with historic Christian principles and character) that we present in this small volume. We believe it to be a paradigm best (if not exclusively) grasped one school—one "community of faith and learning"—at a time.

I was privileged for seven years to serve and now serve again at such a school. As a result, I have observed firsthand the benefits of such an education and have seen my own children and hundreds of others grow in their love both for Christ and for learning. It has delighted me to hear my own children arguing over the proper conjugation of a Latin verb rather than over who gets to play the video game. I swelled with pride when an antique shop owner gave my twelve-year-old daughter a crusty Latin book because she was the only person to ever pick it up and read it (translate it) aloud. I love losing an argument to my son, who has had more formal instruction in logic and classical rhetoric than I can ever hope to acquire on my own. It delights me to read his acknowledgment, now that he has graduated from college, that his liberal arts and sciences primary and secondary education has shaped his life: He "values education and the ability to reason." He "cares about what he has learned." His education "turned him on to things he has learned to love, such as public speaking, persuasion, debate, and reasoning." And it "taught him how to reason and articulate his thoughts so he could persuade others, and be a stronger leader." Most important, as my children have matured into young adults, I have been humbled to recognize deep Christian character in their response to the challenges and even crises they have faced in life.

Fifteen years after the founding of New Covenant Schools in Lynchburg, Virginia, the rigor of the basic curriculum and consequently the average SAT scores there and at similar schools founded since (including those the authors currently serve) tend to exceed the standards for entrance into prestigious colleges and university honors programs. Our students wouldn't mind my saying that they are not geniuses. Like my own children, they are ordinary young people who have had an extraordinary education. It is that education about which we write. That education, expressed in its various forms and contexts, excites us. We are convinced that it provides an extraordinary way, perhaps even the best of a handful of good ways, to educate young people—particularly in today's postmodern culture.

appendix B

The Liberal Arts Tradition in the Public Square: A Historical Apologetic for the Liberal Arts

An authentic liberal arts education relies upon a vast educational civilization that has contended for the minds of students and society for 2,500 years. One key to this kind of education is the goal of shaping students into the right sort of people, equipped with the appropriate knowledge and the right skills for the needs of those around them. A Christian education in the liberal arts should produce citizens who are capable of discerning "the common good," knowing what is merciful and just and leading others toward it.

In America today we face a unique set of challenges in this regard. First, the obvious question: In a pluralistic society like ours, who's to say what is truly just? By what standard do we measure? Second, despite the egalitarian nature of our democracy, many people feel "unempowered" because of the centralization of our government and the various corrupted systems that sustain it. Third, we live in increasingly self-interested times in which the notion of "public service," either through government and military service or through service in church or civic organizations, has fallen out of fashion.

The challenge to Christian educators who are committed to the liberal arts is to cultivate both the skill and the motivation in our students to take on the challenges of leadership in the public square. The history of this educational tradition provides vivid illustrations of how this was accomplished in the past, and it can point us toward the values that should infuse our schools, if we are really serious about culturally relevant Christian education.

For a student to be prepared to shape culture, he must be prepared to understand it. This includes several assumptions: that all cultures are damaged and restricted by the impact of the Fall, that all cultural progress is imperfect and temporary, and that the cultural values of the kingdom of heaven trump all other values that society might impose upon us. At the same time, cultures make better or worse use of biblical notions of truth, goodness, and beauty as the foundations for the traditions that emerge from them. As students study the history of mankind, they need to develop a framework for understanding culture that permits them to distinguish meaningfully between cultures, to evaluate the condition of their own, and to discern what cultures need in order to improve the lots of those who live within them.

Students ought to be prepared and permitted to judge cultures as objectively as possible. If we properly condemn the effective genocide of the Incas by Spanish explorers, we ought also feel free to condemn the same treatment of Native Americans. That the Spanish, having had the benefit of the gospel, might be held to a higher moral standard ought also to enter into that conversation, since the goal of our curriculum is to constantly examine the impact of character and morality on history. It is a shameful sign of our times that non-Christians often consider their secular morality superior to traditional Christian morality because Christians are often unwilling to own up to immoral acts committed under the guise of Christianity.

Ultimately, the key to our students' understanding of culture is a transcendent view based in the cultural values of the kingdom of heaven. A vision of a civilization endowed with justice, mercy, and charity is the vision we want our students to adopt. As they do, we will find them able both to commend and criticize our own present-day context, even as they develop a global vision that submits every culture on our globe to the same evaluative criteria. This same informed global vision will better prepare our wise and eloquent servants to effectively represent Christ's kingdom in their own culture and in others with a winsomeness befitting the gospel and its relevance to every culture under heaven.

While all cultures may not apply Christian values and principles equally, ultimately, in our students' minds, all cultures answer to the same standards of justice, mercy, and charity. With this in mind, let's take a fresh look at the historic contribution of some key cultures to the liberal arts and to our thinking with respect to their application in our own time.

THE HEBREWS

When Moses descended from the mountain at Sinai, he ushered in the age of cooperation between theological and moral convictions and the good of society. All of Hebrew life was ordered by the Law, and the Law made little distinction between religious ritual and civic duty. As God spoke to Moses, he intricately laced the Hebrew's duty to Yahweh together with his duty to every man.

When Jesus summarized the whole Law with the simple maxim, "You shall love the Lord your God with all your heart and with all your soul and with all your strength and with all your mind, and your neighbor as yourself," no carefully observant Jew should have been in the least bit surprised. Provision for the poor, ethical business practices, rights of inheritance, ordinary criminal codes, the rights of immigrants and aliens—all were tied together through the overarching principle of charity. Even though the intrinsic motivation for adhering to the Law was the communal principle of "love" (especially toward God), it was as disinterested a code as existed at the time. It provided no inherent legal advantage to a ruling or religious class, and it assumed that each Hebrew man, woman, and child was essential to society's cohesion around obedience to the Law's statutes. As Hebrew children studied the Scriptures, they could not help but be confronted with the personal responsibility to constantly strive for a just society that would benefit all of its citizens.

Another unique feature of Hebrew culture was that every person was responsible to educate and to be educated in the daily practice and responsibility of the community code. The famous Hebrew *Shema* of Deuteronomy 6, which mandates the continuous tutelage of children in the Law, was given to a wandering horde of former slaves. There was no aristocracy, no landed gentry. For nearly four decades they had been, all of them, at the mercy of God's daily provision of bread from the skies. Even with Moses as their theocratic leader, each Hebrew person stood on identical societal footing, and this seems to be the attitude with which Yahweh wanted them to take possession of the Promised Land.

The education mandate and its pervasive reach into Hebrew society would have even farther-reaching consequences for Hebrew influence in the Near East for the next ten centuries. While Israel would be politically dominant among her neighbors for only brief periods, even in defeat her sons would bear the marks of cultural relevance, inherited from the educated ethos around the study of the Law. When Jeremiah, Ezekiel, and Daniel, for instance, encountered the overwhelming grandeur of Nebuchadnezzar's and Darius's dynasties, their readily observable wisdom and eloquence qualified them, even as conquered peasant peoples, to have a voice in the civic discourse of the monolithic courts. So Jeremiah could legitimately prophesy to the Hebrew exiles living in Babylon, "seek the welfare of the city where I have sent you into exile . . . for in its welfare you will find your welfare." Daniel and his colleagues present themselves as the most acute example of how the Hebrew educational model made itself relevant outside of the comfortable confines of Hebrew society.

So what do Christian educators in the twenty-first century gain from the Hebrew example? First, we are compelled to acknowledge that the secular compartmentalization of our modern educational age is both unbiblical and unhelpful to building whole societies. Second, we can be confident that a biblically oriented education can produce significant cultural contributors, even in a society that acknowledges no biblical reference point. And, third, we face the challenge of ensuring that Christian society is an educated society, and that our educational values and standards are oriented around the law of charity and its impact on the welfare of our own "Babylon."

THE RISE OF FREE PEOPLES

One of the compelling characteristics of the liberal arts tradition is that it has sprung, historically, from circumstances that closely approximate our own as twenty-first-century Americans. The inherent risk of the

American form of government was not lost on the nation's founders or their contemporaries, and its success over the last two hundred years, and especially our rise to global prominence in the last century, would likely have surprised them. They had fashioned the framework for the American experiment on the democratic idealism of the Greeks and the republican sensibilities of the Romans, but the radical democracy of Athens lasted only half a century, and the Roman Republic's golden age lasted less than two hundred years.

Over the centuries, however, the principles that undergirded both have been carefully distilled, co-opted, and reapplied to the educational needs of modern societies. Christians are especially well placed to take advantage of these principles for the benefit of our own modern educational efforts. That is because the church has based most of its educational practices on a constant conviction that biblical Hebrew perspectives on human nature and God's personhood ought to guide and inform proven Greek and Roman approaches to philosophy and education.

Nearly one hundred years after Nebuchadnezzar had sacked Jerusalem, Darius, King of Persia, decided that it was time to head west and expand his empire into Europe. The first stop along the way was the Greek archipelago. A vastly outnumbered army of Athenians met Darius at Marathon. Miraculously, they beat the Hebrew prophet Daniel's adopted sovereign and sent him back to Babylon. Ten years later the Persians under the rule of Xerxes tried again, and thanks to the betrayal at Thermopylae, they breached the combined Greek defenses and poured onto the Peloponnesus. They burned Athens to the ground. The citizens of Athens fled to the hills. They had kept their lives, but their city was ruined, and Athenian civilization teetered on the brink of extinction.

In the ten years between Marathon and Thermopylae, however, the Athenians had shown the foresight to build a navy. Defeated on the ground, the Athenians took to the sea. In the bay at Salamis the Persian navy, recently battered by a storm, was soundly defeated. Xerxes sat on his imperial dais overlooking the battle and watched Persian hopes of conquering Europe quashed once again by upstart farmers who had figured out how to build boats and had learned to sail and then to ram them into other ships and burn them. For the second time in ten years, the Persians retreated back to Persia, this time more or less for good.

Most significantly for our discussion, the liberal arts educational tradition had its beginning in this great conflict between two civilizations, an Asian empire vast in population and resources and a band of Mediterranean farmers and shopkeepers who otherwise would be insignificant to us as modern educators. Given Babylon's military prowess, the Greeks should have been smashed. The Peloponnesus should have been overtaken by Persians, and Europe should have been converted into a western province of the Eastern dynasties. The result could very well have been a Greek civilization characterized by what Daniel describes as one ruled by Babylonian and Persian kings who sought to consolidate their power by creating disproportionate images of themselves. The Athenians might have been relegated to an oppressed, subservient populace whose rulers required their subjects to treat them as if they were deities, exaggerating their place in the world among their own people.

Instead, a new kind of civilization emerged in Athens: a free society characterized by limits and laws rather than by the arbitrary will of rulers who were gods and laws unto themselves. It happened exactly the way that Daniel described in his prophecies. The irony is that Darius, the great king who invades Europe, is at the time being served by this brilliant, aged Hebrew prophet who proclaims that God lifts rulers up and sets rulers down, that God is in control of human history, and that nothing happens apart from his will. It is unnatural to the Christian mind to interpret the Greek story apart from the providence of a personal God who holds sway over the whole of human history. The fortuitous result produced a brilliant flash that has lit most of what has followed in the Western world ever since.

COMMON THEMES WORLDS APART

Defeating the Persians allowed the Greeks to relax a little, and they began to develop an empire of their own. It was far from perfect, but it was distinguished by some remarkable characteristics that would form the basis of many cultures, including our own, for centuries to come. In addition to a set of more or less consistent cultural themes, the educational imperatives that accompany and support these characteristics have formed the basis of Christian education since the time of Augustine. These unique characteristics also laid the groundwork for the Mediterranean civilization into which Jesus would be born and through which his apostles would spread the gospel. From our twenty-first-century vantage point, it is apparent that the whole Mediterranean world had been uniquely prepared for Christ's advent by the separate histories and cultural traditions of their respective civilizations and the subsequent confluence that occurred among them over the centuries just prior to the incarnation.

Both the Hebrews and the Greeks were absolutists—that is, they believed that truth and goodness and beauty are objective values. The Hebrews possessed the superior epistemology in that their certainty relied on divine revelation, but the Athenians' rational dialogues regarding the nature of these three values resulted in a highly sophisticated pedagogical style that Jewish and Christian educators learned to rely on to demonstrate that the things we accept by faith do, in fact, live up to the challenge of rational thought.

The Hebrews and the Greeks also agreed on two basic premises regarding human nature: that human nature is constant and that the human condition is inherently "tragic." The Scriptures describe both the creation and the fall of the whole human race, and the Greeks, while less confident about the precise origin of the human species, were able to deduce that despite all best intentions, despite all best-laid plans, and despite all of our needs for safety and security, the human experience is never quite what is hoped.

Further, despite a strong communal sense in both cultures, Hebrews and Greeks alike held to an extraordinary sense of personal human responsibility. The Hebrew community was bound to God and to each other through the Law, but the prophets made it clear that each person was held responsible not only for his own actions, but for the condition of his own heart before God as well. The Greeks also submitted themselves to a vast cultural and religious tradition, but the ideal of the free conscience held an important place in their assessment of virtue and in their national pride. Nowhere else in the ancient world were people allowed to stand up in public to criticize their rulers. In fifth-century Athens they did it all the time, and sometimes with the astonishing result that the leaders changed their minds or were replaced with people who were more competent or sympathetic.

Another theme common to these two cultures was the cultural

prominence of their literature—especially poetry. The Hebrews were "people of the book," which carried with it the implicit commitment to literacy. Isaiah and Homer were constructing their masterpieces at around the same time period, but Homer was still a blind troubadour, limited by the constraints of collective memories and oral tradition. Isaiah was a scholar from the priestly class, an educated member of the Hebrew literati with the advantage of divine visions and royal libraries. By the fifth century B.C., though, the Greeks themselves were boasting an impressive literacy rate. Playwrights and lyricists were national heroes, regaling their fans in annual play competitions designed to honor the gods, and political oratory had become the city-state's most famous industry.

As classicist Louise Cowan has said, "The two fountainheads of poetic wisdom for the West have been the Greek and Hebrew writings. One speaks of nobility, the other of humility. Both are necessary. And in both it is primarily in poetry that they communicate their hearts and enable us to find our own."[1]

We derive heroism from the Greeks, humility from the Hebrews. Christian humanists from Augustine to Erasmus to Cardinal Newman have contended for centuries that this combination of Greek and Hebrew qualities is what makes our culture so unique.

Heroism, especially military valor, exists as a value in virtually every culture. But the Greeks championed the cause of individual freedom and the independence of every person's conscience under law. The Greek city-states were free societies, governed by laws, and threatened on all sides by "barbaric" cultures that did not recognize the supremacy of law or the value of self-determination. This self-determining spirit provides the basis for all liberal democracies and is the envy of all those who live under tyrannies of every kind.

But the Greeks erred in positioning mankind at the center of the cosmos, calling him the measure of all things. The corrective to this presumption is the Hebrew contention, expressed in the law of Moses and in the prophets' diatribes, that man, made in God's image, lives under his authority and is liable to his judgment. The Hebrews were taught to "walk humbly with [their] God" who holds the whole world in his hands and whose purpose and will mankind is obligated to pursue.

The fusion of Greek and Hebrew ideals produced an explosion of ideas, combined together in remarkable ways and lived out in extraordinary stories of human achievement. Heroism and humility blended together in the first century A.D. to define a new kind of hero—the martyr. People were burned alive or torn to pieces by animals, humbly refusing to surrender to the government under which they lived, gallantly standing firm in faith and in the hope of their own resurrections.

The humble hero pervades these poetic traditions and provided the framework for legends based on chivalric values of selfless courage and piety. Leaders in the modern world could stand a lesson or two from this heritage, but very few schools teach that these historic values of heroism and humility have much relevance in the technologically savvy, global economy.

THE CRISIS

But we get ahead of ourselves. Let's turn our focus again to Athens in the fifth century B.C. and to the rise of the liberal arts. As democracy took hold in the most prominent Greek city, virtually all spheres of civic life were under its control, including the courts. Athens became a very litigious society, especially as the internecine Peloponnesian Wars dragged on and economic and political pressures increased. There were no prosecutors in the Athenian justice construct, no justice department, no police. The citizens enforced the law among themselves and against each other. In order to be successful in court, one had to be skilled in the law, in arguments, and in oratory. There was no legal representation, and this resulted in the need for people to be educated in order to represent their own legal interests.

To meet the need for preparing ordinary citizens to protect themselves in court, a class of professional educators called *rhetors* came into existence to train laypeople in the arts of legal persuasion. As moderns, we think of presenting a case in court as something one does maybe once in a lifetime. But fifth-century Athenians may have appeared in court several times within the space of a year. The *rhetors* (sometimes called *sophistes* or "wise ones") set up schools, and it was not long before ordinary citizens began to make "rhetoric," or the art of persuasive discourse, a fundamental aspect of each child's education.

There were other reasons for training in oratory. Virtually all of the affairs of the government, from levying taxes to waging the seasonal wars against Sparta, were decided by popular votes. Everything had to be deliberated, contested, and decided in public. Each citizen was empowered with the responsibility to contribute to public debates and to cast votes, which would determine the courses of action for the state. But as the century dragged on and Athenian life became more contentious, litigation in open courts became the dominant focus of educators' priorities. Before long rhetoricians developed the reputation for caring very little about whether or not a case was just or true, and the terms *sophists* and *sophistry* took on negative connotations. The rhetoricians came to be known as illusionists who made just arguments seem unjust and unjust arguments just, turning truth on its head to get one's way in court. The corruption of the courts indicated deeper societal corruption. By the time Athens finally succumbed to the Spartans' relentless warring, democracy had collapsed and tyranny had taken hold.

The historical symbol of Athens' rapid decline is the death of Socrates in 399 B.C. He was convicted in a sham trial, in an environment very much like those just described. His execution sounded the death knell of the Athenian democracy. It also provoked a violent and influential reaction from Socrates' most famous student, Plato, who envisioned a utopia in which the rhetoricians are all dead, and only philosophers (dialecticians) are left to lead commerce and govern society. Plato contended that rhetoric and morality were completely incompatible, as the tyranny of having one's way through persuasion would always overpower ethical sensibilities. The practice of the liberal arts was being called into question on moral grounds, and the fledgling tradition's relevance was in serious jeopardy.

WISDOM AND ELOQUENCE EMERGE

The struggle between philosophers and rhetoricians in early fourth-century B.C. Athens was a battle for the Hellenic soul.[2] Plato railed against rhetorical convention in a series of dialogues designed to expose the moral naivete of rhetoric and to champion speculative philosophy as a paradigm for leadership in the crisis-ridden state.[3] As might be expected, Plato's *Socrates* insists that knowledge is essential to goodness and that rhetoric, as being devoid of content, cannot inform genuine virtue without the guidance of philosophy.

As Plato's thought matured, he would eventually propose a political structure that practically does away with rhetoric. In its place, dialectic would become the commercial language of philosopher-kings, whose rational inquiry into the ideal forms of civilization would lead to a nonpolitical utopia in which all matters of state would become obvious to those who are adequately endowed with dialectic acumen. There would be no need for persuasion, as "the best" in every circumstance would be virtually self-evident.

While Plato harangued the sad state of rhetoric, Isocrates, a brilliantly successful teacher of oratory, stepped up to its defense. Something of a progressively minded conservative, Isocrates reached back to take hold of the dependable Greek principle of moderation to chart a course through the moral quagmire of post-Golden Age Athens. As one historian described Isocrates' goal:

> The essential was to find a mean, as it were, between the moral indifference that had previously characterized rhetorical education, and the Platonic resolution of all politics into morality, which from a practical point of view was going to lead away from all politics. The new rhetoric had to find an ideal which could be ethically interpreted and which at the same time could be translated into practical political action.[4]

Isocrates understood that the Greek way of independent thinking and action risked extinction if the self-interested forces that had so radically relativized the moral landscape were not checked. He proposed a new type of educational program that would include dialectic as a means to a more fitting rhetoric. A system of rhetorical forms was called for, by which students of rhetoric might more simply analyze and respond in various rhetorical contexts.

Having systematized this analytical element, Isocrates insisted that the task of the orator is not complete until he has injected his own literary imagination into the process. "Perfect eloquence," Jaeger summarizes, "must be the individual expression of a single critical moment . . . and its highest law is that it should be wholly appropriate."[5] How to determine the appropriateness of such expression continues to perplex both rhetoricians and philosophers to this day.

The importance of the debate between the fourth-century B.C. philosophers and rhetoricians is that it points out that while the liberal arts tradition has held supreme status in Western educational systems, it has never been without controversy. Further, from the beginning the most critical dimension of the controversy was that of the moral appropriateness of the discipline: Can rhetoric be adopted as a device to train young citizens to keep the best interests of their audiences in mind as they practice their craft? Isocrates represents the beginning of a middle way between the demagoguery of the sophists and Plato's unworkable abstractions. But his is only one of many rhetorical middle ways between the poles of opposing political or philosophical factions.

As to the question of moral character training, the mandate would remain that orators must learn their trade in the context of what constitutes *moral* appropriateness. While this understanding does vary in time and place, as each culture or subculture defines its notion of "the highest good," we can determine whether that culture's orators are learning to employ rhetoric in the consistent pursuit of this value. Even so, as Christian teachers and parents work to construct schools designed to encourage the pursuit of the biblical "highest good," those schools can evaluate the usefulness of rhetoric in the students' experience of that pursuit.

More than any other inhabitant of the classical world, Augustine devised a *via media* between the various extremes that confront an educated Christian. Most famous for his defense of Christian orthodoxy against early heresies, the great African bishop also blazed an educational path that brought philosophy and rhetoric together as inextricable allies in nurturing wisdom and eloquence.

A native of North Africa, Augustine had been trained in the mid-fourth century A.D. as a Ciceronian orator. At a young age, he was promoted within academic circles and became a highly regarded professor of rhetoric at Milan. It was there that he encountered the oratorical power of the Christian bishop Ambrose and where he was eventually converted to Christianity.

Because of the autobiographical transparency of his writing, it is a simple thing to reconstruct the philosophical and rhetorical influences that shaped Augustine's thinking. In addition to Cicero and other Stoic philosophers, the young Augustine would certainly have encountered the philosophy of Quintilian, history's first public educator, who served the Roman emperor Nero and was one of the most important practitioners of rhetoric as a tool for articulating the moral obligations of the orator in society. It was Quintilian who first called the educated person "the good man speaking well."

A quick summary of Quintilian's thinking on the subject might help to show the way in which Augustine connected pagan classical thinking about leadership to his own Christian theories of persuasion and the responsibilities of educated Christians. First, Quintilian demands that any definition of "orator" include a moral component. In Quintilian's mind, a self-serving rhetorician is a rhetorician in name only. In saying so, he disallows any mental packaging that ignores the corrosive effect of private immorality upon the orator's public leadership, a problem that we Americans seem to face in every generation.

Second, to Quintilian, "excellence of character" requires a social ethic. Every person's thinking and behavior affects the shape of society at large. So whether one conducts oneself honorably in business will have a profound effect upon the nobility of the culture one is helping to shape. Quintilian's code of ethics requires that each person weigh the effect that his or her behavior will have on others.

Third, the perfect orator is expected to affect his society directly. In the Roman Imperium, this was a role reserved for the senatorial and equestrian classes. In republican democracies such as America's, however, significant roles in public discourse are more common than many think. Our legal system depends upon the participation of conscripted jurors with no formal training in law, our election system depends upon the participation of voters with little political experience, and our educational systems (public and private) often invite the participation of those with little more than their own basic schooling as credentials. Add to that the popularity of congregationally governed churches and civic organizations, and the average person will spend most of his adult life engaged in activities that require persuasive input. This universality of application makes the character of the orator an issue of primary importance in today's world.

By the fifth century A.D., Augustine defined the conversation regarding the Christian appropriation of rhetoric as a *via media* between wisdom and eloquence (*sapientia et eloquentia*). As Christianity encroached on Roman paganism in the fourth century A.D., eventually being institutionalized by Constantine as the official state religion, the relationship between the Christian gospel and rhetoric was more and increasingly highly contested. Rhetoric, for good reason, had been understood to be a pagan discipline—after all, who were its promoters? Moses and the prophets had little use for soothing and appealing methods of persuasion. Paul himself repeatedly rejected the sophistic tradition and asserted divine authority as the basis for his mission and livelihood, as in saying to the Corinthians that "we are not, like so many, peddlers of God's word, but as men of sincerity, as commissioned by God, in the sight of God we speak in Christ" (2 Corinthians 2:17).

Three hundred years after Paul's death, Augustine found himself the preeminent leader in a church beset by hostile paganism as well as considerable complacency within her own doors. In his famous *On Christian Doctrine* (or *Teaching*), he describes the role of Christian thinking as the Roman Empire was unraveling. The Christian religion having been legitimized by decree, Augustine's concern is not so much the conversion of pagans as it is the motivation of the nominal parishioners whom he finds frequently inhabiting his churches. To this end, motivating the weak in faith to live in a way characterized by bold authentic belief, he engages the Christian *rhetor*, or "the expositor and teacher of the Divine Scripture."[6]

The Christian rhetorician must be "the defender of right faith and the enemy of error, should both teach the good and extirpate the evil."[7] To this end, he is fully obligated, even if, in the pursuit of truth, the Christian rhetorician might pay less attention to eloquence than his audience prefers. The first requirement of the expositor/teacher, and one of Augustine's important concessions in favor of a practical rather than a philosophical rhetoric, is that he be "wise, if not eloquent."[8]

Eloquence, Augustine argues, can be learned by imitation, and the principles of effective oratory, as helpful as they might be, need not be memorized—especially if the study of rhetoric competes with the study of the Bible. After all, the principles of eloquence were not invented by men but, rather, discovered, much like the principles of mathematics. Effective speech is effective speech, no matter how sophisticated the analysis or the conceptualization of what makes it so.[9]

Augustine, much like Aristotle, is intent upon the practical outcome of rhetoric more than he is concerned with the adherence to strict form. "The speaker," he chides, "should not consider the eloquence of his teaching but the clarity of it."[10] He quotes Cicero in reference to this as saying that some of the more skilled orators understand that effective persuasion sometimes requires "a kind of studied negligence" that rejects more elegant forms of speech in favor of simpler prose that the audience easily grasps.[11] In rhetorical theory, this attitude qualifies Augustine as a very modern-thinking man, and Calvin, the first of the modern Christian theologians, would later pick up this rhetorical theme in his own stylistic formula of *claritas et brevitas* (clarity and brevity).

But still, the necessity of rhetoric prevails in Augustine's thinking, since the greatest task of the Christian expositor/teacher[12] is to move his hearers to faith-filled responsibility. It is not enough, then, just to teach truth, if the effect is that the audience simply gains knowledge without being motivated to loving action (cf. Paul's assertion that "knowledge puffs up, but love builds up," 1 Corinthians 8:1). He even goes to the extent of ascribing a curious definition to the verb "to speak," so that he claims that the teacher who speaks without being understood has not really spoken. "On the other hand," he maintains, "if he is understood, he has spoken, no matter how he has spoken [i.e., eloquently or otherwise]."[13] Again he quotes Cicero: "To teach is a necessity, to please is a sweetness, to persuade is a victory."

Perhaps most important to the debate over rhetoric's place in Christian thought, Augustine persistently insists upon the use of the mind in the exercise of spiritual service and the necessity of an educated clergy. "If anyone says that if teachers are made learned by the Holy Spirit they do not need to be taught by men what they should say or how they should say it, he should also say that we should not pray because the Lord says, 'for your Father knoweth what is needful for you, before you ask him,' or that the apostle Paul should not have taught Timothy and Titus what or how they should teach others."[14]

For an outline of this instruction, Augustine again turns to "the author of Roman eloquence," Cicero. Already having referenced Cicero regarding the relationship between teaching, delighting, and persuading, Augustine adds the Ciceronian principle of "appropriateness." "He therefore will be eloquent who can speak of small things in a subdued manner, of moderate things in a temperate manner, and of grand things in a grand manner."[15] He expands this principle by combining the two trilogies together:

He is therefore eloquent who
In order to teach, can speak of small things in a subdued manner,
And in order to please, can speak of moderate things in a temperate manner,
And in order to persuade, can speak of great things in a grand manner.[16]

In the end, Augustine's assessment of the Christian rhetorician's responsibility reflects the whole of the classical tradition of rhetoric beginning with Aristotle: "it is the universal office of eloquence . . . to speak in a manner leading to persuasion: and the end of eloquence is to persuade of that what you are speaking. . . . If [the eloquent man] does not persuade, he has not attained the end of eloquence."[17]

Augustine directs a Christian liberal arts pedagogy in several significant ways. First, he understands that the orator must maintain a primary obligation to truth. As both Quintilian and Cicero observed, the orator who is unconcerned with truth and justice is a charlatan. In Augustine's case, however, pagan philosophy has been replaced by the Christian gospel. Philosophy no longer bears the responsibility of discerning ultimate truth through the utilization of naked reason, but its role is now to harmonize and synthesize the truth of the Scriptures with the dialectical and rhetorical methods of the classical philosophers and orators.

Second, Augustine confirms classical rhetoric as an accurate conceptualization of effective, persuasive speech and the dialectical component of invention as helpful to the task of the Christian teacher.[18] Though he questions the necessity of learning all that the Greek and Roman orators have to say on the subject in order to effectively orate, Augustine does not contest at any point the accuracy of Aristotle's or Cicero's observations on rhetoric. Further, he does not distinguish between "classical" and "Christian" rhetoric, but the formerly pagan orator sees the pagan paradigm for understanding to have been superseded and co-opted by the Christian worldview.

Third, Augustine represents a middle way between unconscious dependence upon either authoritative revelation or pure reason in the persuasive effort. *On Christian Doctrine* does not describe "the rhetoric of persuasion" as a means of proselytizing.[19] Augustine is clear elsewhere that conversion is entirely dependent upon the prevenient grace of God's Spirit. Still, the task of motivating lethargic believers to live energetic lives of faith falls largely to the rhetorician who knows the Scriptures and will use his oratorical skill to motivate his audience. So, in tandem with his predestinarian theology, Augustine maintains that human oratory is a critical means by which God accomplishes his will in the world.

Fourth, Augustine affirms the ethically minded classical rhetoricians in his insistence that the "good man" will be the best orator. Characteristically, though, his view of the relationship between morality and effective speech is not so absolute as Quintilian. Stoicism, as a natural theology devoted to the perfectibility of human nature, imposed a legalistic totality that Christianity rejects.[20] Augustine is clear that righteous men will be the most persuasive orators,[21] but at the same time he allows that audiences do not have the means to discern every motivation of the speaker, and "thus they benefit many by preaching what they do not practice; but many more would be benefited if they were to do what they say."[22]

He concludes with a typically humble challenge, reflective of the Hebrew ethos: "Whether one is just now making ready to speak . . . or is composing something to be spoken later . . . or to be read, . . . he should pray that God may place a good speech in his mouth . . . and for the profitable result of their speech they should give thanks to him from whom they should not doubt they have received it, so that he who glories may glory in him in whose hand are both we and our words."[23]

In short, Augustine provides the Christian educator with a basis for confidence in the liberal arts tradition. If our goal is to provide the church and the watching world with confident, competent, selfless leaders, the liberal arts constitute a dependable path toward that goal. Augustine represents the grace with which God has repeatedly gifted our civilization: the ability to blend the blessings of special revelation (the truth of the Scriptures) with the blessings of common grace (the liberal arts educational paradigms). The result is our ability as modern Christian teachers to envision our students influencing the world around them for the good of all of us.

appendix C

THE ALIGNED COMMUNITY: PURPOSE AND PLANNING

THE SCHOOL COMMUNITY comprises students and teachers, administrators and support staff, board members and parents, the churches represented by the student body, and the school's friends who support the mission by contributing time and money. Within each of these groups we might find dozens of different ways that people describe the school. Usually these perspectives are somewhat harmonious. It is not uncommon, however, for people to believe things about a school's identity and mission that are just not true. For a Christian school to effectively pursue its mission of producing wise and eloquent graduates, it must be an aligned community.

Alignment can be defined as like-mindedness about the essential qualities of the school and a common understanding that everything that happens under the school's banner is informed or required by its core mission. We often use the term "vertical alignment," or the insistence that every activity, every decision, flows figuratively downhill from the school's mission. A vertically aligned school can be confident that each member of the community understands the school's mission and his or her role in helping to achieve that mission.

Conscious alignment frees people to work in the school's interests. Not too long ago a strategic planning consultant sat around a conference table with a school's board of directors and their new head. The previous head had been terminated early in the previous school year, and the reaction had produced chaos. A board member had been forced to resign, a senior administrator lost her job, and parents were in an uproar. Divisions within the board were stark, and the air was thick with suspicion. The first step toward planning a successful future for the school might have seemed to revisit previous disagreements and resolve them. But a more important task was proposed. "Let's go around the table," the consultant prodded, "and listen as each person describes the purpose of this school." Several hours later, the group unanimously endorsed the school's historic mission and determined to craft a plan that could make that mission a reality. The personal divisions and political turmoil the school had just experienced suddenly seemed unimportant as compared to the vision that the mission provided for the future.

The practice of rearticulating and reevaluating the school's mission needs to be a regular occurrence. The goal of this discussion is to constantly solidify agreement and support from all of the community's stakeholders around the school's essential character and to regularly evaluate how well the benefits of these essentials are being expressed in the school.

THE OPEN COMMUNITY

In the old days, private schools often operated like private clubs. A domineering headmaster with a board of chummy insiders set the identity, tone, and direction of the school for each generation of students. Most of the schools' constituents were passive consumers of the school's culture and had little interest in or opportunity to contribute to the shape of the institution.

No longer. In today's collaboratively minded society, in which technology moguls wear jeans to work and politicians set policy by polls, a tight-fisted, centralized approach to setting a school's course and culture feels constraining and counterintuitive to most parents. At the same time, as more and more Christian schools talk about the parental responsibility to educate their children as a basic value, we create the expectation among parents that the school should honor parental prerogatives.

These expectations can obviously come into conflict with basic institutional realities. Parental involvement in the leadership structures of schools, and the personalized interests that accompany that involvement, can create real challenges to the organizational and administrative stability of a school. Facing those challenges with a leadership structure that includes a wide variety of stakeholders and that helps to ensure loyalty to the school's mission above personal interests can be tricky, but it is absolutely necessary.

Collaboration requires openness. This means openness to the evolution and broader application of the school's mission. It means openness to a wide variety of people with the interest and talent to serve the school. It means open access to decision-making processes. It means openness to a broad constituency, each of whom loves something different about the school. But openness often is perceived to work against institutional controls and efficiency. That leaves the basic question that boards and administrators need to ask: Are we willing to give up some of the traditional control we've had of our school in favor of a high degree of ownership from the whole community?

Several crucial elements can contribute to the successful management of this tension. First, the school's mission must be regularly promoted and reviewed. It is not uncommon for a school's recruitment and admissions messages to be full of references to the global ideals contained in the mission. But too often once a family is admitted, they hear very little about the effect that the school's transcendent values are having on their children daily.

Second, parents can be given responsibility to promote the school's mission to other parents—from parents' perspective. Parents who are well educated in the unique characteristics of the school's culture and community (what are the liberal arts? what difference does it make to educate students with worldview objectives in mind?) and who are perceptive enough to notice the difference the school makes in their own children ("you wouldn't believe the conversation we had at dinner the other night!" "Let me tell you what my son learned by persevering through that tough Latin class last year") trump any other promotional effort we can mount.

Third, teachers and staff can be trained to view parents as partners in the school's mission, and parents can be trained to respect the important institutional responsibilities that teachers and staff contend with every day. Too often school communities lose the benefits of openness because we force ourselves to choose between parental prerogatives or institutional values. The inevitable results of this false dichotomy can be seen in schools in which parents feel free to invade any space within the school and to insist on their own interests or in schools in which the staff excludes parents except for fund-raising activities. Relationships between parents and the professional staff that are characterized by the recognition of boundaries and a biblical sense of mutual submission are not natural. They must be encouraged and modeled by the school's leadership.

Fourth, a school, and especially boards and administrators, must be willing to consider changes to the ways in which the historic mission is achieved or applied to the community. Traditions are a wonderful part of every great school's culture, but traditional ways of doing things (or not doing things) can sometimes be confused for the mission itself. Progressively thinking parents, economic changes, and competition for like-minded families can all be sources of innovative ideas to expand the school's reach and the shape of the community.

THE PLANNED COMMUNITY

A community characterized by openness needs a structure that points its members toward the mission, communicates the school's current priorities clearly, and helps organize conversations about the future and the consideration of new ideas. Disciplined, ongoing, strategic planning provides a constant reference point for members of the school community who want to know where the school is headed and why.

Columbia, Maryland, midway between Washington, D.C. and Baltimore, was one of the nation's first "planned communities." The genius of this approach to city planning was the concept that quality of life issues should dictate how a city is built and managed. With that non-negotiable principle driving the planning process, Columbia developed a feeling of organization, security, and convenience that many suburban cities didn't have. A school's strategic plan must also be vertically aligned to the school's mission. Everything starts with the school's stated purpose for existence and flows down from there. If an idea or activity cannot be justified within the framework of the school's purpose, it should not be planned. When strategic plans are directly connected to the school's purpose, every discussion about strategic priorities or action items is an opportunity to reinforce the essential identity that everyone in the community needs to support.

A legitimate strategic planning process should also include as many of the school's stakeholders as possible in order to achieve broad ownership for the identity and direction of the school. Most schools that engage in strategic planning typically involve the governing board and senior administration in the process, but a school that views itself as a larger, aligned community seeks involvement from faculty, staff, students, parents, key contributors, and even civic or corporate leaders.

Resistance to a collaborative approach to planning often arises from the fear that peripheral stakeholders will run away with "our school" and make it something that "we don't want it to be." Typically, though, including the broader constituency in a carefully crafted, vertically aligned process helps focus the whole community on the essential issue of faithfulness to the school's purpose, and this allows the school's leadership to mine a larger collective experience for a richer, more accurate expression of the community. People who have participated meaningfully in a strategic planning process emerge as legitimate owners of the school's mission. Our own experience in starting schools confirms that as schools grow, the original vision expands as the community grows. As more and more people buy into the mission and contribute to the school's future, exclusive control by a few forceful personalities becomes less and less necessary.

Successful strategic planning also requires persistence. Countless organizations have invested time, energy, and money in strategic plans that serve only to collect dust on shelves. Strategic planning is a dynamic, ongoing process that requires constant evaluation and accountability. Its greatest benefit is to organize the myriad activities within a school around central themes, but those themes and activities have to be constantly tested to ensure that they are supporting and expanding the reach of the school's purpose. This ongoing effort requires discipline and focus. Board meeting agendas may need to be abbreviated to give sufficient time to discuss longer-term priorities. Staff reports may need to be reorganized to reflect attention to planning priorities and to update regular progress. Parent or stakeholder meetings may need to be held at regular intervals, both to report on the strategic planning progress and to ascertain which ideas about the school's future are gaining currency among families. Depending on how comprehensive the planning process is, extra staff may need to be hired or additional duties assigned to keep documentation current and to ensure accountability to priorities that the planning process dictates.

Strategic planning methods have multiplied over the past two decades as corporate America has come to grips with the competitive realities of the global economy and the need for a company's business objectives to be both certain and highly adaptable. Most schools do not face the same global pressures, but the effort that business has put into this area of management certainly can be used as we plan. An approach called Appreciative Inquiry is a research-based approach to managing organizational change that begins by asking stakeholders what they appreciate about the organization. As they strategize ways to build on the organization's strengths, the organization's "identity capital" (the strength of its essential characteristics) "appreciates" (increases in value in people's minds and in the priorities that are set for growth). In this approach, a trained facilitator[1] determines, through interaction with a core group, the essential questions to be addressed in the process. Then time is devoted to actively engaging the whole community—both as a "committee of the whole" and in break-out subgroups to address questions and to work toward consensus on a handful of core identity statements or strategic action items.

Whether the planning employs a formal process like Appreciative Inquiry or not, the goal ought to be to figure out what strengths a school possesses and how to capitalize on those strengths. Often leaders are tempted to allow problems or shortcomings to set the agenda for strategic plans. The result is a to-do list intended to offset perceived deficits, but very few of the items on a list like that will expand the application of the school's mission and identity. A school's core strengths need nourishment. Planning that focuses on weakness will solve some problems, but the school's basic identity suffers from neglect, leaving stakeholders little in which to invest.

A workable strategic plan needs several layers of ideas and documentation. A list of action items with dates and assignments is important, but these need to be clearly aligned to the school's mission by intermediate goals. The higher up within the structure of the strategic plan a goal is stated, the less likely that it will be changed. Lower level action items can be subject to change at any moment, depending on circumstances. Boards and administrative teams that are committed to disciplined planning learn to negotiate how all of this works.

At Regents School of Austin, ten "Strategic Objectives" have been adopted that define the shape of all of the school's plans.[2] On the school's strategic planning organization chart, these ten objectives reside just below the school's mission. They consist of a clear expression of how the Regents community plans to achieve the mission to which they have committed themselves. We are not suggesting that every school have ten strategic objectives, but the point is that there are not that many. They are easy to summarize and even to commit to memory, and everyone in the school, from faculty to students to parents, bumps into them regularly. Once these largely non-negotiable objectives are set, the school is ready to define additional principles that will promote the achievement of the major objectives. Several levels down from the Strategic Objectives are goals and action items for which board members, faculty, administrative staff, and parent committees have real ownership.

Once a framework for strategic planning is in place, the real work begins. The relevance and power of a strategic plan boils down to its execution. Execution requires faith in the wisdom of the plan, concentration on the plan as a guide for priorities and resources, and the right people in place to manage the ongoing demands of the plan.

Faith in a school's plan comes from several sources. First, if the school's constituency feels included in the plan's origin, people are likely to consider it a reflection of their own perspectives and values. Likewise, leaders who have been primarily responsible for the plan's development must heartily endorse and stubbornly support the plan. In a school in which members rotate on and off the board or key committees, it is essential that new members be indoctrinated into the strategic plan and that they be equipped to promote it.

A plan has no effect if leaders forget that it exists or if they neglect to use it to guide decisions. The strategic plan should have the effect of simplifying many decisions by providing a clear sense of priority to the decision-making process. Boards and staff must constantly discipline themselves to use the plan as a constant reference point in determining courses of action for the school. The ongoing relevance of the plan requires constant maintenance of the plan's documentation and dissemination. A school board that cares about strategic planning must also care that the plan is carefully maintained and updated. Because this work is often very detail-oriented and routine, it might make sense for a competent staff person other than the head to manage the plan's oversight. However the job is distributed, strategic plans must be conscientiously maintained in order to make an ongoing positive impact.

AUTHORITY IN THE ALIGNED COMMUNITY

Strategic plans are often looked at as a ready answer to the question, "What are we doing?" But a well-conceived, well-maintained planning process can help schools address other persistent questions as well.

One of the stickiest issues facing private schools is the relationship between the governing board and the administration, especially the school's head. Usually tension in this relationship boils down to a question of authority—who's in charge of what, and who has the final say on decisions that need to be made? Many schools have seen their institutional wheels come off because of conflict that arises over competition for authority. Mismanagement of this tension is also one of the key reasons that average tenures of private school heads are at an all-time low.

Suggested solutions to this issue range from the oversimplified to the absurdly complex. Some suggest that all conflict is a matter of people's hearts. If people were genuinely committed to the biblical attitudes of humility and mutual submission, some say, conflicts would not exist because every circumstance or decision could be negotiated out through transparent dialogue. This may be true in some contexts, but this perspective usually cannot account for the practical realities that growing organizations face multitudinous decisions requiring authority or that in healthy organizations people must be assigned jobs and must be held accountable to do them. All the humility in the world won't tell a board or an administrative team who is best equipped to do something or how it should be done.

Other solutions to tension over authority run along the lines of centralizing the majority of decision-making powers to a board. "Parent-run" or "board-run" schools are increasingly popular and are typically administered by a central committee that considers all aspects of the school's administration with scrutinizing attention to detail. In these structures, staff and teachers have little genuine authority as every decision they make in the classroom or in the office is open for review and revision at the discretion of the board. It is no wonder that schools that organize this way often have difficulty recruiting and retaining qualified, capable professionals.

Competition for authority is a natural state of affairs in organizations ordinarily created by two competing interests.[3] First, if a school's governing board is doing its job well, it will be concerned with institutional controls that preserve and promote the school's mission, require the employment of talented people who believe in the school's mission, prescribe admissions policies that assure like-mindedness in the community, monitor the quality of each student's experience, ensure fiscal responsibility, provide for adequate facilities . . . the list of fiduciary responsibilities can seem endless. Active, attentive boards sense the deep responsibility they have for each member of the community and the future of the school.

The second element of this tension over authority comes as talented, capable professional staff become invested in the school's mission and want to see it expanded and developed in ways that correspond to their knowledge, experience, and personalities. Wise boards would rather hire "broncos" who need bridling than "burros" who need to be driven toward excellence. Two active parties, boards and heads, who inhabit substantial overlapping space are bound to step on one another's toes.

Working through the distribution of authority in a Christian school begins with a Christian understanding of the nature of authority itself. The Scriptures teach that we live in a hierarchical universe. All authority is ordained by God, and every Christian has a moral responsibility to obey the authority over him. Administrators and teachers all live under the legitimate authority of governing boards who are the school's "owners" by virtue of their fiduciary responsibility for the legal corporation. This might sound somewhat formal, but the authority that boards possess in schools is identical to the legal authority that civil governments possess in cities and countries, just applied to the mission of Christian education. The governing body of a school possesses all authority within the community.

This conclusion runs against common understandings of school administration that divide authority into spheres, as if there were a set of natural laws that assign some authority to boards, some to professional staff, some to parents. Depending on which governance manual or educational consulting theory one subscribes to, the divisions may differ, but the basic principle is constant.

This position on authority also means that boards who abuse their authority by treating staff unethically or discourteously and staff who compete with their boards for authority that does not rightly belong to them are each behaving un-Christianly. This may seem to be a strong statement, but if authority means something in our worldview, and it must, then there are real moral implications regarding the ways in which authority is both used and submitted to.

But we have already criticized governing boards who insist on maintaining a tight hold on authority. So what are we proposing? Miriam Carver, of the Carver Institute on Policy Governance, has described the board's management of its authority this way: It is a board's responsibility to figure out how much authority it can possibly give away within the school community and to establish accountability measures that assure that it can give authority away confidently and comfortably.[4] Practically speaking, a board should never insist on keeping authority regarding jobs or decisions that can be better handled by someone else. The prudent distribution of authority within the school, combined with carefully constructed accountability, assists efficiency and productivity throughout the school.

The wise distribution of authority includes one significant condition that every board should impose on itself in order to avoid confusion and the possibility of offending capable staff and parents. The authority that the board possesses is a collective authority. It does not reside in any individual, but only in the board as a whole, when it acts legally as a whole. Boards that allow individual members to act authoritatively within the school community, as if they possess the authority of ownership, set themselves up for potentially bitter conflicts with staff, teachers, and parents whose own delegated spheres of authority will be invaded. Generally a board's collective authority outside the boardroom is the authority that they vest in the school head, but strict parliamentary guidelines for a board's exercise and delegation of its authority are a necessary component of an aligned community.

The well-designed strategic planning process, combined with prudent governing policies, organizes the conversation about who will be responsible for what and how success will be measured. Heads of school that are invested in strategic planning with their boards have the opportunity to think along with the board as authority is distributed comfortably. Once authority is distributed, either through standing policies or through the ongoing planning process, a board's job is to observe the boundaries it has established and to let people do their jobs. A head's job is to continue to distribute authority throughout the school community, to other administrators, to faculty, to parents, and to students, and to hold each group or person accountable for the proper use of that authority to achieve strategic goals.

NOTES

CHAPTER 1

1. Plato, *The Republic*.
2. Augustine, *On Christian Doctrine* (New York: The Liberal Arts Press, 1958).
3. John Dewey, *Freedom and Culture* (Buffalo, NY: Prometheus Books, 1989).

CHAPTER 2

1. *De Architectura*, I, 1, 12, as cited in *The Catholic Encyclopedia* online (www.new advent.org/cathen).
2. *Didascalicum*, III, 3, as cited in *The Catholic Encyclopedia* online (www.new advent.org/cathen).
3. *The Catholic Encyclopedia* online (www.newadvent.org/cathen).
4. Plato, *The Republic*.
5. *Doctrinale*, XVII, 31, as cited in *The Catholic Encyclopedia* online (www.new advent.org/cathen).
6. Dorothy L. Sayers, *The Lost Tools of Learning* (New York: National Review, 1947).
7. *Didascalicum*, VI, 3, as cited in *The Catholic Encyclopedia* online (www.new advent.org/cathen).

CHAPTER 3

1. Peter S. Heslam, *Creating a Christian Worldview: Abraham Kuyper's Lectures on Calvinism* (Grand Rapids, MI: William B. Eerdmans, 1998).
2. Francis A. Schaeffer, *How Should We Then Live?* (Old Tappan, NJ: Fleming H. Revell, 1976).
3. Wilhelm Dilthey, *Introduction to the Human Sciences: An Attempt to Lay a Foundation for the Study of Society and History* (Detroit: Wayne State University Press, 1989).
4. *Nouthesia* involves interrupting the formal instruction to spontaneously model godly wisdom through individual or whole class guidance, correction, or discipline when opportunities arise.
5. Heslam, *Creating a Christian Worldview*.
6. John Calvin, *Institutes of the Christian Religion*, 2 vols. Trans. Ford Lewis Battles. Ed. John T. McNeill (Philadelphia: The Westminster Press, 1960).

CHAPTER 5

1. Appreciative Inquiry is an organizational development/management tool that capitalizes on maximum stakeholder participation in driving positive change. See www.appreciativeinquiry.org.
2. In this regard, Sayers indicates that the Kings and Queens of England could do nicely, but for American students other benchmarks will prove more appropriate. New Covenant Schools in Lynchburg, Virginia, instituted one of the first K-12 "historical literacy" programs, helping young students master a chronological list of key events and dates

through the incorporation of verbal and kinesthetic mnemonic devices. Tapes and transcripts of the so-called Grammar of History are available from New Covenant Schools.

CHAPTER 6

1. While we strongly advocate the development and utilization of memory skills, we unequivocally reject the use of memory as a substitute for the development of other essential learning skills.

2. Orton and Guillingham's methods have been adapted to the classroom by several of their protégés and, in turn, by the protégés' associates. Among the more common of these are the Spalding and Riggs methods.

3. Great Books Foundation, *A Manual for Co-Leaders* (Chicago: Great Books Foundation, 1965).

4. Jessie Wise and Susan Wise Bauer, *The Well-Trained Mind* (New York: W.W. Norton, 1999).

5. Romalda Bishop Spalding and Walter T. Spalding, *The Writing Road to Reading* (New York: William Morris and Company, 1990).

6. We use "reconstruction" here in its original sense of constructing an objective and believable sense of past events through a scholarly analysis of the available records.

7. Critical Thinking Press provides some materials that are helpful in this regard; www.brightminds.us/home/index.jsp.

8. Web site: http://www.aclclassics.org/.

9. Aristotle, *On Rhetoric*. Trans. George A. Kennedy (New York: Oxford University Press, 1991).

10. Classical rhetoric employs three types of appeal that correspond to the ancient Greek— *logos, pathos, ethos*: rational appeal, emotional appeal, ethical appeal (or the appeal to the speaker's character). Others, like Lunsford and Ruszkiewicz, have added appeals based on "values" as a fourth option with particular relevance in a pluralistic society.

CHAPTER 7

1. Richard Restak, M.D., *The New Brain* (New York: Holtzbrinck Publishers, 2003).

2. Ibid.

CHAPTER 8

1. Cicero, *De Oratore*. Trans. E. W. Sutton and H. Rackham. 2 vols. The Loeb Classical Library (Cambridge: Harvard University Press, 1948), I.v.17-18.

2. Vickers, quoting Henri Marrou, who maintains that despite the detailed conventions of the *progymnasmata* "the [student] artist had complete freedom within the system, and when he had mastered the various processes he could use them to express his own feelings and ideas without any loss of sincerity. Far from hindering originality or talent, the restrictions enabled very subtle, polished effects to be produced." *In Defence of Rhetoric* (Oxford: Clarendon Press, 1988).

3. Rhetorical forms are divided into five "canons": Invention (the discovery of arguments), Disposition (the arrangement of arguments), Elocution (style of composition), Memory, and Presentation (or pronunciation).

4. See Edward P. J. Corbett and Robert J. Connors for a comprehensive treatment of the

role topics play in formal persuasive discourse. *Classical Rhetoric for the Modern Student*. Fourth edition (New York: Oxford University Press, 1999), 84-130.

5. Treated separately, Aphthonius addresses refutation first. It makes sense that it is easier for students to critique the arguments of others before attempting to formulate their own. However, as confirmation typically precedes refutation in formal discourse, and since Aphthonius' treatment of the two exercises is nearly identical, we have reversed his order.

6. On this count, recall how one learns mathematics or a foreign language (especially a classical language). Conscientious teachers, to the students' dismay, always require that math students "show their work" along with the correct answers, and they require that language students, regardless of the fluency of the students' prose, can parse the words they have translated.

7. Augustine employs an argument along these lines (*On Christian Doctrine* [New York: The Liberal Arts Press, 1958], II.27) where he uses Varro's account of the origin of the Nine Muses and their naming by Hesiod to argue against the notion that the love and learning of music is corrupted by the pagan claim that the Muses were begotten by Jupiter.

8. In Aphthonius, these two exercises are treated separately but similarly. Between Confirmation/Refutation and Praise (ἐγκώμιον)/Blame, Aphthonius also inserts the exercise called Commonplace. The essence of this exercise is to argue against some great evil in reference to the life of one representatively evil person (e.g., to argue against racism in the prosecution of James Earl Ray or against disloyalty in the prosecution of Alcibiades).

9. Aphthonius prescribes three stylistic exercises: comparison, characterization, and description. As comparison and characterization contain a strong dialectical element, I have included them in the modern *progymnasmata*. Description lacks a substantial dialectical element and is almost entirely stylistic. We shall leave description to the teachers of general composition.

CHAPTER 9

1. Quintilian, *Institutio Oratoria*. 4 vols. Trans. H. E. Butler. The Loeb Classical Library (Cambridge, MA: Harvard University Press, 1996).

2. David Perkins, *Smart Schools* (New York: The Free Press, 1992), 8.

3. Developed by Henry Stein, copyright 1997 by Alfred Adler Institute of San Francisco.

4. Keep in mind that *preliminary exercises* to the study of rhetoric ought to begin at a very young age, but this is not to be confused with the start of formal rhetorical studies that cannot reasonably precede some formal training in logic.

5. Louis Auchincloss, *The Rector of Justin* (New York: Houghton Mifflin, 1988).

6. Augustine, *On Christian Doctrine* (New York: The Liberal Arts Press, 1958).

CHAPTER 10

1. Dorothy L. Sayers, *The Lost Tools of Learning* (New York: National Review, 1947).

2. David Perkins, *Smart Schools* (New York: The Free Press, 1992), 7.

3. Mortimer J. Adler, *The Paideia Program* (New York: Macmillan, 1984).

4. Perkins, *Smart Schools*.

5. E. D. Hirsch, Jr., What Your _____ Grader Needs to Know series.

6. Howard Gardner, *The Disciplined Mind* (New York: Penguin Books, 2000), 81.

7. E. D. Hirsch, Jr., editor, *The Core Knowledge Series: Resource Books for Grades One Through Six* (New York: Doubleday, 1991).

8. New Covenant Schools in Lynchburg, Virginia, instituted a "12-K" historical literacy program, requiring students to master a cumulative list of facts that followed them through their schooling.

9. Mortimer J. Adler, *The Paideia Proposal* (New York: Macmillan, 1982).

10. Some sophisticated grammar programs, like Shurley Grammar, increase the ability of young students to analyze sentences by requiring them to memorize syntactical patterns to which they then orally apply formulaic questions, dissecting the sentences one word at a time—a very sophisticated cognitive skill broken down into a mnemonic form.

11. Quintilian's phrase to describe the goal of education.

12. Adler, *The Paideia Proposal*.

APPENDIX A

1. E. D. Hirsch, Jr., *Cultural Literacy: What Every American Needs to Know*. New York: Houghton Mifflin, 1987).

2. Stanley Hauerwas and John H. Westerhoff, *Schooling Christians* (Grand Rapids, MI: William B. Eerdmans, 1992).

APPENDIX B

1. Louise Cowan, "The Necessity of the Classics," *The Intercollegiate Review*, Fall 2001.

2. As Werner Jaeger put it: "From this point on, the rivalry of philosophy and rhetoric, each claiming to be the better form of culture, runs like a *leitmotiv* throughout the history of ancient civilization" (*Paideia: The Ideals of Greek Culture*. 3 vols. Trans. Gilbert Highet [New York: Oxford University Press, 1944], 3:46).

3. According to George A. Kennedy, the real Gorgias' response to this dialogue was, "How well Plato knows how to satirize!"—perhaps a sign of how seriously the rhetoricians of the day took the philosophers' polemics (*Classical Rhetoric and Its Secular and Christian Tradition from Ancient to Modern Times* [Chapel Hill, NC: University of North Carolina Press, 1980], 45).

4. Jaeger, *Paideia*, 3:53.

5. Ibid., 3:61.

6. That this notion has the potential to do violence to rhetoric as an overarching paradigm for learning is evidenced by some Renaissance rhetoricians, such as Rudolf Agricola who asserted that "the first and proper objective of speaking is to teach" (Kennedy, *Classical Rhetoric and Its Secular and Christian Tradition from Ancient to Modern Times*, 208). Teaching, to Agricola, consists primarily of exposition and arguments, which positions rhetoric as a minor subset of dialectic. In this economy, and others like it, rhetoric is reduced to elementary style, while the effectiveness of speech begins to be understood to be nearly exclusively mathematical/logical.

7. Augustine, *On Christian Doctrine* (New York: The Liberal Arts Press, 1958), IV.6.

8. Ibid., IV.7.

9. Ibid., IV.4.

10. Ibid., IV.23.

11. Ibid., IV.24.

12. Kennedy associates exegesis and teaching (hermeneutics and homiletics) with Aristotle's dialectic and rhetoric (*Classical Rhetoric and Its Secular and Christian Tradition from Ancient to Modern Times*, 58).

13. Augustine, *On Christian Doctrine*, IV.27.
14. Ibid., IV.33.
15. Ibid., IV.34.
16. We have added the versified format to point out the alliterative quality. For a technical explanation of these three styles see the pseudo-Ciceronian *Ad Herennium*, Book IV, especially viii-xi.
17. Augustine, IV.55, IV.34.
18. "For since by means of the art of rhetoric both truth and falsehood are urged, who would dare to say that truth should stand in the person of its defenders unarmed against lying, so that they who wish to urge falsehoods may know how to make their listeners benevolent, or attentive, or docile in their presentation, while the defenders of truth are ignorant of that art?" (ibid., IV. 3).
19. Kennedy, *Classical Rhetoric and Its Secular and Christian Tradition from Ancient to Modern Times*, 157.
20. Compare Augustine also to Aristotle's emphasis on the ethical appeal: "[There is persuasion] through character (εθος) whenever the speech is spoken in such a way as to make the speaker worthy of credence. ＊ . And this should result from the speech, not from a previous opinion that the speaker is a certain kind of person . . . character is almost, so to speak, the controlling factor in persuasion" (2.4).
21. "The life of the speaker has greater weight in determining whether he is obediently heard than any grandness of eloquence" (IV.59).
22. Ibid., IV.60.
23. Ibid., IV.63.

Appendix C

1. We heartily endorse the use of experienced educational or strategic consultants, especially in the early stages of a school's strategic planning process. An objective third party is less constricted by assumptions and biases that should be challenged in the process, he or she has no personal interests to conflict with larger institutional concerns, and a third party allows controversial topics to be addressed without those topics being associated with a board member's or administrator's or parent group's "agenda."
2. Regents's first five Strategic Objectives pertain to students' experience around the key concepts of student discipleship, teaching a Christian worldview, a liberal-arts-based curriculum, developing cultural leaders, and engaging parents with the responsibility for their own students' education. A second set of five Strategic Objectives focuses on institutional best-practices in governance and leadership standards, leadership for like-minded schools, business plans, access to families from a broad socioeconomic spectrum, and quality facilities. These ten objectives cover virtually any category of concern or suggested activity that might arise.
3. Keep in mind that the Christian worldview requires us to acknowledge basic self-centeredness as the ultimate source of conflict, but we believe that even as individuals learn to acknowledge and restrain their self-interests in certain circumstances, avoidable conflict will arise if it is promoted by the school's decision-making structures.
4. Paraphrased from an unpublished lecture at the Society for Classical Learning conference in June 2005.

BIBLIOGRAPHY

Adler, Mortimer J., *How to Speak How to Listen*. New York: Simon & Schuster,1983.

_____. *Paideia Problems and Possibilities*. New York: Macmillan, 1983.

_____. *The Paideia Proposal*. New York: Macmillan, 1982.

_____. *The Paideia Program*. New York: Macmillan, 1984.

Aphthonius, "Progymnasmata." *Rhetores Graeci*. Ed. Leonhard Spengel. Vol. 2. B.G. Teubneri, 1854.

Aristotle, *On Rhetoric*. Trans. George A. Kennedy. New York: Oxford University Press, 1991.

Augustine, *Against the Academicians* and *The Teacher*. Trans. Peter King. Indianapolis: Hackett Publishing, 1995.

_____. *On Christian Doctrine*. New York: The Liberal Arts Press, 1958.

_____. *On Christian Teaching*. Trans. R. P. H. Green. New York: Oxford University Press, 1997.

_____. *The City of God*. New York: Random House, 2000.

Baldwin, Charles Sears, *Ancient Rhetoric and Poetic*. New York: Macmillan, 1924.

_____. *Medieval Rhetoric and Poetic*. New York: Macmillan, 1928.

Barbe, Walter B., and Raymond H. Swassing, *Teaching Through Modality Strength: Concepts and Practices,* Columbus, OH: Zaner-Bloser, Inc, 1979.

Barzun, Jacques, *Begin Here*. Chicago: The University of Chicago Press, 1991.

_____. *Teacher in America*. Indianapolis: Liberty Press, 1981.

Bauer, Susan Wise, *The Well-Educated Mind*. New York: W. W. Norton & Company, 2003.

Bennett, William J., Chester E. Finn, Jr., and John T. E. Cribb, Jr., *The Educated Child*. New York: The Free Press, 1999.

Blamires, Harry, *The Christian Mind*. Ann Arbor, MI: Servant Publications, 1963.

Bloom, Harold, *The Western Canon*. New York: Harcourt Brace and Company, 1994.

_____. *Where Shall Wisdom Be Found?* New York: Riverhead Books, 2004.

Boice, James Montgomery, *Two Cities, Two Loves*. Downers Grove, IL: InterVarsity Press, 1996.

Bolt, John, *The Christian Story and the Christian School*. Grand Rapids, MI: Christian Schools International, 1993.

Braaten, Carl E. and Robert W. Jenson, *The Two Cities of God: The Church's Responsibility for the Earthly City*. Grand Rapids, MI: William B. Eerdmans, 1997.

Brown, Colin, *Christianity and Western Thought*, Vol. 1. Downers Grove, IL: InterVarsity Press, 1990.

Brown, Peter, *Augustine of Hippo*. Berkeley: University of California Press, 1967.

Bunting, Josiah, III, *An Education for Our Time*. Washington, D.C.: Regnery Publishing, 1998.

Cahill, Thomas, *How the Irish Saved Civilization*. New York: Doubleday, 1995.

Calvin, John, *Institutes of the Christian Religion*. 2 vols. Trans. Ford Lewis Battles. Ed. John T. McNeill. Philadelphia: The Westminster Press, 1960.

Chadwick, Henry, *Augustine*. Oxford: Oxford University Press, 1986.

Cicero, *Rhetorica Ad Herennium*. Trans. Harry Caplan. The Loeb Classical Library. Cambridge: Harvard University Press, 1989.

Cicero, *De Oratore*. Trans. E. W. Sutton and H. Rackham. 2 vols. The Loeb Classical Library. Cambridge: Harvard University Press, 1948.

_____. *On Moral Obligation (De Officiis)*. Trans. John Higinbotham. Berkeley: University of California Press, 1967.

Cooperrider, David L., Peter F. Sorensen, Jr., Therese F. Yaeger, and Diana Whitney, *Appreciative Inquiry*. Champaign, IL: Stipes Publishing, 2001.

Corbett, Edward P. J. and Robert J. Connors, *Classical Rhetoric for the Modern Student*. Fourth edition. New York: Oxford University Press, 1999.

Crider, Scott F., *The Office of Assertion*. Wilmington, DE: Intercollegiate Studies Institute, 2005.

DeKuyper, Mary Hundley, *Trustee Handbook*. Seventh edition.

Washington, D.C.: National Association of Independent Schools, 1998.

Dewey, John, *Freedom and Culture*. Buffalo, NY: Prometheus Books, 1989.

_____. *How We Think*. Amherst, NY: Prometheus Books, 1991.

Dilthey, Wilhelm, *Introduction to the Human Sciences: An Attempt to Lay a Foundation for the Study of Society and History*. Detroit: Wayne State University Press, 1989.

Drucker, Peter F., *Managing the Non-Profit Organization*. New York: HarperCollins Publishers, 1990.

Durant, Will, *The Life of Greece*. New York: Simon & Schuster, 1939.

Gaebelein, Frank E., *A Varied Harvest*. Grand Rapids, MI: William B. Eerdmans, 1967.

Gardner, Howard, *The Disciplined Mind*. New York: Penguin Books, 2000.

Great Books Foundation, *A Manual for Co-Leaders*. Chicago: Great Books Foundation, 1965.

Gregory, John Milton, *The Seven Laws of Teaching*. Grand Rapids, MI: Baker Book House, 1995.

Gutek, Gerald L., *A History of the Western Educational Experience*. Prospect Heights, IL: Waveland Publishers, 1987.

_____. *Cultural Foundations of Education*. New York: Macmillan, 1991.

Hauerwas, Stanley and John H. Westerhoff, *Schooling Christians*. Grand Rapids, MI: William B. Eerdmans, 1992.

Heslam, Peter S., *Creating a Christian Worldview: Abraham Kuyper's Lectures on Calvinism*. Grand Rapids, MI: William B. Eerdmans, 1998.

Hicks, David V., *Norms and Nobility*. Lanham, MD: University Press of America, 1999.

Highet, Gilbert, *The Art of Teaching*. New York: Vintage Books, 1989.

Hirsch, E. D., Jr., *Cultural Literacy: What Every American Needs to Know*. New York: Houghton Mifflin, 1987.

_____., ed. *The Core Knowledge Series: Resource Books for Grades One Through Six*. New York: Doubleday, 1991.

Holmes, Arthur F., *Ethics*. Downers Grove, IL: InterVarsity Press, 1984.

_____. *The Making of a Christian Mind*. Downers Grove, IL: InterVarsity Press, 1985.

WISDOM *and* ELOQUENCE

Huntington, Samuel P., *The Clash of Civilizations and the Remaking of World Order*. New York: Simon & Schuster, 1996.

Jaeger, Werner, *Early Christianity and Greek Paideia*. Cambridge, MA: Harvard University Press, 1961.

_____. *Paideia: The Ideals of Greek Culture*. 3 vols. Trans. Gilbert Highet. New York: Oxford University Press, 1944.

Joseph, Sister Miriam, *The Trivium*. Ed. Marguerite McGlinn. Philadelphia: Paul Dry Books, 2002.

Jowett, B., *Plato's The Republic*. New York: Random House, 1950.

Kennedy, George A. *Classical Rhetoric and Its Secular and Christian Tradition from Ancient to Modern Times*. Chapel Hill, NC: University of North Carolina Press, 1980.

_____. *Quintilian*. New York: Twayner Publishers, 1969.

_____. *The Art of Persuasion in Greece*. Princeton, NJ: Princeton University Press, 1963.

Kopff, E. Christian, *The Devil Knows Latin*. Wilmington, DE: Intercollegiate Studies Institute, 1999.

Kuyper, Abraham, *Lectures on Calvinism*. Grand Rapids, MI: William B. Eerdmans, 1999.

Lewis, C. S. *Mere Christianity*. New York: MacMillan, 1960.

_____. *The Abolition of Man*. New York: Simon & Schuster, 1947.

Luce, Tom and Lee Thompson, *Do What Works*. Dallas: Ascent Education Press, 2005.

Lunsford, Andrea and John J. Ruszkiewicz, *Everything's an Argument*. Third edition. Boston: Bedford/St. Martin's, 2004.

Marrou, H. I., *A History of Education in Antiquity*. Trans. George Lamb. Madison, WI: The University of Wisconsin Press, 1956.

McNeill, John T., *Calvin: Institutes of the Christian Religion 1*. Philadelphia: The Westminster Press, 1990.

_____. *Calvin: Institutes of the Christian Religion 2*, Philadelphia: The Westminster Press, 1990.

Niebuhr, H. Richard, *Christ and Culture*. New York: Harper and Row, 1951.

O'Donnell, James J., *Augustine*. New York: HarperCollins, 2005.

_____. *Avatars of the Word*. Cambridge, MA: Harvard University Press, 1998.

Ornstein, Allan C. and Daniel U. Levine, *Foundations of Education*. Fourth edition. Boston: Houghton Mifflin, 1989.

Palmer, Parker J., *The Courage to Teach*. San Francisco: Jossey-Bass, 1998.

Perkins, David, *Smart Schools*. New York: The Free Press, 1992.

Plato. *Collected Dialogues*. "Republic." Trans. Paul Shorey. Ed. Edith Hamilton and Huntington Cairns. Princeton, NJ: Princeton University Press, 1961.

Postman, Neil, *The End of Education*. New York: Vintage Books, 1996.

Quintilian, *Institutio Oratoria*. 4 vols. Trans. H. E. Butler. The Loeb Classical Library. Cambridge, MA: Harvard University Press, 1996.

Ravitch, Diane, *Left Back*. New York: Touchstone Books, 2000.

Restak, Richard, M.D., *The New Brain*. New York: Holtzbrinck Publishers, 2003.

Sayers, Dorothy L., *The Lost Tools of Learning*. New York: National Review, 1947.

Schaeffer, Francis A., and Udo Middelmann, *Pollution and the Death of Man*. Wheaton, IL: Crossway Books, 1970.

Schaeffer, Francis A., *Death in the City*. Downers Grove, IL: InterVarsity Press, 1969.

_____. *How Should We Then Live?* Old Tappan, NJ: Fleming H. Revell, 1976.

_____. *The God Who Is There*. Downers Grove, IL: InterVarsity Press, 1976

_____. *True Spirituality*. Wheaton, IL: Tyndale House, 1971.

Schall, James V., *Another Sort of Learning*. San Francisco: Ignatius Press, 1988.

Simmons, Tracy Lee, *Climbing Parnassus*. Wilmington, DE: Intercollegiate Studies Institute, 2002.

Sowell, Thomas, *Inside American Education*. New York: The Free Press, 1993.

Spalding, Romalda Bishop and Walter T. Spalding, *The Writing Road to Reading*. New York: William Morris & Company, 1990.

Veith, Gene Edward and Andrew Kern, *Classical Education*. Washington, D.C.: Capital Research Center, 2001.

Vickers, Brian, *In Defence of Rhetoric*. Oxford: Clarendon Press, 1988.

Watkins, Jane Magdruder and Bernard J. Mohr, *Appreciative Inquiry*. San Francisco: Jossey-Bass, 2001.

Weston, Anthony, *A Rulebook for Arguments*. Third edition. Indianapolis: Hackett Publishing Company, 2000.

Wilder, Amos N., *Early Christian Rhetoric*. Cambridge, MA: Harvard University Press, 1971.

Wilson, Douglas, *Recovering the Lost Tools of Learning*. Wheaton, IL: Crossway Books, 1991.

_____. *The Case for Classical Christian Education*. Wheaton, IL: Crossway Books, 2003.

_____. *The Paideia of God*. Moscow, ID: Canon Press, 1999.

Wise, Jessie and Susan Wise Bauer. *The Well-Trained Mind*. New York: W.W. Norton and Co., 1999.

Woodruff, Paul, *First Democracy*. New York: Oxford University Press, 2005.

www.brightminds.us/home/index.jsp.

www.newadvent.org/cathen.